COMBAT AIRCRAFT

146 JUNKERS Ju 188 UNITS
OF WORLD WAR 2

SERIES EDITOR TONY HOLMES

146

COMBAT AIRCRAFT

Robert Forsyth

JUNKERS Ju 188 UNITS OF WORLD WAR 2

OSPREY

PUBLISHING

OSPREY PUBLISHING

Bloomsbury Publishing Plc

Kemp House, Chawley Park, Cumnor Hill, Oxford, OX2 9PH, UK

29 Earlsfort Terrace, Dublin 2, Ireland

1385 Broadway, 5th Floor, New York, NY 10018, USA

E-mail; info@ospreypublishing.com

www.ospreypublishing.com

OSPREY is a trademark of Osprey Publishing Ltd

First published in Great Britain in 2022

A catalogue record for this book is available from the British Library.

ISBN; PB 9781472836380; eBook 9781472836373; ePDF 9781472836366; XML 9781472836397

22 23 24 25 26   10 9 8 7 6 5 4 3 2 1

Edited by Tony Holmes
Cover Artwork by Gareth Hector
Aircraft Profiles by Janusz Światłoń
Index by Zoe Ross
Originated by PDQ Digital Media Solutions, UK
Printed and bound in India by Replika Press Private Ltd

Osprey Publishing supports the Woodland Trust, the UK's leading woodland conservation charity.

To find out more about our authors and books visit **www.ospreypublishing.com**. Here you will find extracts, author interviews, details of forthcoming events and the option to sign up for our newsletter.

Front Cover

In one of the last offensive missions carried out by Ju 188s in force, in the early evening of 21 April 1945 eight A-3 variants from III./KG 26 led by Hauptmann Friedrich-Wilhelm Gehring, the *Staffelkapitän* of 7. *Staffel*, joined ten Ju 88s of II./KG 26 on an armed reconnaissance to the east coast of Scotland. Taking off from their Norwegian base at Stavanger, to where they had transferred in readiness for the mission from Bardufoss and Trondheim, all aircraft were loaded with torpedoes which they were to use against shipping between the Orkneys and the Firth of Forth. The formation flew in two waves, in line astern, in loose *Ketten*, with the Ju 188s of III. *Gruppe* in the second wave at a little over 300 m above the sea.

Gareth Hector's cover artwork portrays one of the Ju 188s in its typical 'meander' or scribble pattern camouflage applied for overwater operations. The aircraft is seen fitted with antennas for the FuG 200 'Hohentwiel' search radar, and it would probably have been loaded with a pair of LT 5FB torpedoes as depicted here.

As described in Chapter Four of this book, the mission was to prove a costly one for the Junkers' crews, including the loss in one Ju 188 of a holder of the Knight's Cross following an encounter with RAF Mosquitos

Previous Pages

The neat, in-flight profile of Ju 88 V44 Wk-Nr 1687 NF+KQ is seen to advantage here. It is fitted with BMW radials mounted to a new, longer wing design with more pointed tips, but still carrying dive brakes and a newly designed tail assembly. The aircraft is armed with a 20 mm MG 151 cannon and two 13 mm MG 131 machine guns (*EN Archive*)

CONTENTS

CHAPTER ONE

DESIGN AND DEVELOPMENT

For good reason, the name 'Junkers' is synonymous with German inter-war and wartime aviation. During the 1920s and 1930s, the Junkers Flugzeugwerke based in the Saxony–Anhalt town of Dessau, at the junctions of the Mulde and Elbe rivers, built a series of all-metal aircraft, including the single-engined F 13 (the world's first metal airliner) and several other successful, if short-lived, commercial machines. The F 13 saw service in more than 30 countries, while the firm's later, larger, three-engined G 24 won international recognition when two examples made a long-range, route-proving flight from Berlin, across Siberia, to the Far East.

The corrugated Duralumin with which Junkers built its early aircraft proved a very suitable material, and although parasitic drag was more of a problem than with smooth skins, it was not too much of an issue when considering the relatively low aircraft speeds of the time. This philosophy eventually manifested itself in the Ju 52/3m airliner/transport, which would serve as a beacon for German aeronautical design, engineering and reliability. For several years, as a result of the Ju 52/3m, the German national airline Deutsche Luft Hansa became one of the best in the world, trailblazing routes across Europe and in South America, South Africa and the Far East.

With the outbreak of World War 2, the Ju 52/3m proved itself a sturdy, dependable multi-role transport for the Luftwaffe. It went on to serve on

A wind tunnel model of the Ju 85 project from the late 1930s showing a long, tapered fuselage, twin vertical stabilisers (to aid installation of rear guns), ventral gondola and raised cockpit canopy. Although not connected directly to the Ju 188, it would serve as inspiration to *Dipl.-Ing.* Ernst Zindel when he worked on that design (*EN Archive*) every front to which German forces were deployed, becoming respected by its crews and army ground units whenever the latter became trapped in 'pockets' by enemy forces. The Ju 52/3m was also critically important when supplies of fuel, food, ammunition and spares had to be flown across the Mediterranean or the vast, open and dangerous spaces of Soviet Russia. Finally, the aircraft airlifted more wounded troops from the battlefronts to safe rear-area hospitals than any other Luftwaffe transport.

Another Junkers design also gained a reputation as an iconic (to use an overused, but in this case quite accurate term) symbol of German *Blitzkrieg*. The inverted gull-winged Ju 87 was a purpose-built dive-bomber that made its operational debut with the Luftwaffe's *Legion Condor* in Spain's catastrophic civil war. Despite initial scepticism amongst some senior German air commanders, the Stuka was used to devastating effect when pinpoint accuracy was required against Republican positions and ships.

With tactical experience gained in Spain, the Ju 87 went on to specialise in attacking similar targets in Poland, the West, the Balkans, North Africa and the USSR, its howling dive-bombing earning the aircraft a fearsome reputation amongst enemy forces. Quite literally, the Ju 87 was the airborne spearhead that offered effective battlefield support to German ground forces during their offensive campaigns between 1939 and 1942.

But perhaps most superlative of Junkers' leading designs was the Ju 88, a type which has become regarded as one of the outstanding combat aircraft of World War 2. Entering service in the autumn of 1939 as a *Schnellbomber* (fast bomber), the sleek Ju 88 soon came to be regarded as the most advanced bomber in the world.

It had evolved from a series of prototypes created during the 1930s by a formidable team of designers and engineers at Dessau under the leadership of *Dipl.-Ing.* Ernst Zindel. They had responded to a 1934 requirement from the *Reichsluftfahrtministerium* (RLM – German Air Ministry) for a multi-role and heavily armed '*Kampfzerstörer*' ('battle destroyer') that would be able to fly bomber, reconnaissance and ground-attack missions.

Just months later, however, the RLM revised its requirement as it was envisaged that, realistically, such an aircraft would be viewed as '*Es kann alles, aber nichts davon richtig*' (a 'Jack of all Trades, but a Master of None'). Thus the requirement was focused towards a *Schnellbomber* with a crew of three, which would be able to climb to 7000 m in 25 minutes, fly at a maximum speed of 500 km/h and carry a maximum bombload of 1000 kg on horizontally mounted racks to a range of around 2000 km. The aircraft was to be ready quickly – by August 1935. To ensure speed in performance, the *Schnellbomber* would be either unarmed or carry the minimum armament in the belief that, with such power and lightness, it would easily be able to evade attack from any enemy fighter.

The tender for such a specification was put out to the firms of Focke-Wulf, Henschel, Junkers and Messerschmitt. Although the August 1935 deadline came and went, work began on prototypes in May 1936, and what emerged from the Zindel team was a twin-engined, low-wing design with a single fin and rudder. The crew was accommodated in a 'greenhouse' cockpit positioned well forward and housed beneath a canopy that was almost flush with the fuselage. Power came from a pair of 1000 hp

Daimler-Benz DB 600A 12-cylinder, liquid-cooled engines housed in neat, slim nacelles. The first all-metal, stress-skinned prototype, the Ju 88 V1, took to the air from Dessau on 21 December 1936.

By 1938 the competing firms had eased out of the tender, and Junkers was officially awarded the task of building the *Schnellbomber*. On 3 September of that year, Commander-in-Chief of the Luftwaffe, Generalfeldmarschall Hermann Göring, told *Dr.* Heinrich Koppenberg, the head of Junkers, 'Go ahead and give me a great bomber fleet of Ju 88s in the shortest possible time!'

Indeed, so elated and confident was Generalmajor Ernst Udet, the head of the *Technisches Amt* (Technical Department), with Junkers' work on the Ju 87 that in November 1937 he had ordered that the Ju 88 should also be built with dive-bombing capability, thus adding another major requirement to its 'multi-role' tasks. Zindel duly brought in his colleague, *Dipl.-Ing.* Herrmann Pohlmann, who had worked on the Stuka, to incorporate a dive brake system into the Ju 88 so as to ensure the aircraft would be able to pull out safely from dives.

In its most notable earliest offensive deployment in the spring of 1940, the Ju 88 gave a good account of itself as a bomber against British warships anchored in Scapa Flow, and it was regarded confidently as another shining symbol of Nazi technical accomplishment and superiority.

Powered by two supercharged 1200 hp Jumo 211B-1 12-cylinder, liquid-cooled, fuel-injected engines that produced a maximum speed of 450 km/h at 5500 m, the Ju 88A-1 could, on paper, carry a bombload of 1400 kg, comprised of 28 50-kg SC 50 bombs. Put another way, the aircraft could carry 500 kg of bombs for 3677 km with fuel tanks full, but on shorter missions of up to 1260 km, it could carry 2400 kg of bombs. The crew of four was protected by a windscreen-mounted 7.9 mm MG 15 machine gun. Two further such guns were mounted in the rear of the cockpit and at the rear of a ventral fuselage gondola.

Following, with some delay, from the A-1, the A-2 (Jumo 211G engines) and the A-3 (dual-control trainer), the Ju 88A-4 started to enter service in 1940. It featured some major design improvements, and additions, including the fitment of new Jumo 211Js rated at 1350 hp which had finally become available, and an extended wingspan of 20.08 m, compared to the A-1's 18.25 m. A number of A-1s were modified to A-4 standard through the addition of the new wing, with these aircraft being designated A-5s – a variant that actually preceded the A-4 marginally when examples were delivered

The Ju 88 was a superlative, multi-role combat aircraft, first seeing action in 1939, and serving through to the end of the war, having undergone a series of redesigns and modifications. More than 15,000 examples had been built by war's end. Here, groundcrew work on the port-side Jumo engine of a Ju 88A-1 or A-4 at an unidentified forward airfield. The Ju 188 would be based on the Ju 88 airframe (*Author's Collection*)

in the spring of 1940. Nevertheless, it would be the A-4 that would go on to equip many Luftwaffe bomber and reconnaissance units, and remain in service for the entire war, earning itself a formidable reputation in the process.

Eventually, more than 15,000 Ju 88s would be built by 1945 in a range of variants and for different roles, including bombing, day and nightfighting and photo- and weather-reconnaissance, making it the most widely produced twin-engined type in the Luftwaffe inventory. But the origins of what became the Ju 188, essentially a derivative of the Ju 88, lay in the latter's extensive prototype development programme, although initial impetus was largely maintained by private initiative on the part of Junkers.

During the early phase of development of the Ju 88, under the coordination of Zindel as Head of Construction, together with *Dipl.-Ing.* Heinrich Hertel as the firm's Head of Technical and Aircraft Development, a new variant was proposed to follow the A series which would offer improved range, reduced drag (thus increased speed) and greater ordnance payloads.

It is believed that the origins of, and inspiration for, the new variant lay in the Ju 85 project of late 1936, overseen by two members of Zindel's team, Wilhelm Evers, who had worked for the Fokker Aircraft Corporation of America, and Alfred Gassner, an Austrian who had earlier been employed by the Fairchild Corporation in the USA. The Ju 85 was considered a candidate for the RLM's 'Bomber A' programme – a requirement issued on 3 June 1936 for a new, long-range, heavy bomber suitable for waging independent strategic air warfare but also capable of diving attacks.

'Bomber A' was to weigh 27 tonnes, have a range of 5000 km and a speed of 500 km/h at 5500 m. The aircraft was to be powered by four engines, each of around 1000 hp, of either the Daimler-Benz DB 601 or Jumo 211 12-cylinder liquid-cooled in-line type, the Jumo 206 six-cylinder diesel, the BMW 139 or Bramo 329 14-cylinder air-cooled radials, or the Argus As 412 14-cylinder liquid-cooled in-line. The aircraft was to be able to take off, overloaded if necessary, within 1000 m. It was further decreed that the bomber should be capable of carrying the heaviest types of ordnance. 'Bomber A' would be operated by a crew of three, made up of two pilots, one of whom would command the aircraft and operate one of its defensive guns, and a radio operator/gunner.

The Ju 85 never progressed beyond the wind tunnel model and mock-up stage. Larger than the Ju 88 airframe that came later, it underwent several modifications in shape. The aircraft had a twin tailfin arrangement, and its two sets of coupled Daimler-Benz engines were identical in layout to the Ju 85's 'Bomber A' rival, the Heinkel He 177. These features suggest a different intended requirement for the Ju 85 when compared to the Ju 88. However, Zindel did prepare a B series of the Ju 85, which, unlike the initial Ju 88 prototypes and the A series, incorporated a tall, raised, fully glazed, bulbous canopy over its spacious cockpit area, as well as a ventral cupola.

Initial efforts by the Junkers design team to develop the successor to the Ju 88A series – the B (*Berta*) – commenced in 1937. The design centred to a great extent on reducing drag, and it was felt that this could best be achieved by a major redesign of the forward fuselage, as well as more streamlined and aerodynamically shaped engine nacelles, bomb racks and dive brakes. Thus, the B series saw the standard cockpit area of the Ju 88A replaced by a bulbous and bulged structure, with increased and extensive glazing fitted into a heavily frameworked construction, and the removal of the standard stepped windscreen. To the rear, the canopy ran down towards the fuselage to a neatly faired gun position. It was estimated that by introducing such features, along with more power, maximum speed could increase by almost 100 km/h over the Ju 88A.

While internally emulating the crew accommodation of the Ju 88A, Hertel intended the innovative and highly advanced new cockpit design as an all-round vision unit offering the best possible conditions for combat operations. The underside of the forward section was also bulged to carry a ventral, rearward-firing machine gun. All in all, a little more internal space was found without the need to widen the cockpit section.

Initially, however, the RLM viewed this as too radical a change to an established design, and it was of the opinion that for the foreseeable future the Ju 88A was adequate for the bomber tasks required of it. More than that, there was a need for a sufficient number of bombers 'immediately' so as to prosecute the coming war effectively. In a swipe at the Luftwaffe's Do 19 and Ju 89 four-engined bomber types, Göring was apparently heard to remark, 'The *Führer* does not ask me how big my bombers are, but how many there are'.

This sentiment is echoed by what General der Flieger Erhard Milch, State Secretary at the RLM, told Major im Generalstab Paul Deichmann, Chief of the Luftwaffe's Air Command Leadership Branch, in early 1937. 'Milch declared that all available industrial capacity was needed for the production of Ju 88s', Deichmann recalled, and that 'the much vaunted advantages of the four-engined bomber were far overrated, both in Germany and abroad. The development of the four-engined bomber, even for limited production as test models, would endanger the Ju 88 programme'.

Eventually, in 1939, the proposed B series was 'officially' re-evaluated, not just incorporating a new cockpit section, but with the intention of fitting the anticipated and ultimately scarce 1500 hp Jumo 213A bomber engine or, (initially) as an alternative, the 1550 hp BMW 139. Interchangeability was an important factor, as was the ability to co-produce the series alongside the Ju 88A, although it was decreed by the RLM that work should continue on a semi-official basis only, which, in reality, indicated a low priority on the part of the ministry.

In June, the RLM issued an official order for four 'experimental' (as distinct from prototype) aircraft to be designated the V23 through to the V26 which were to be completed as soon as possible. Furthermore, a mock-up of the cockpit was constructed with full internal fittings, although this was different in shape to

The Junkers employees sitting in the pilot's and observer/bomb-aimer's seats of this Ju 88B forward-section mock-up lend a sense of scale. Here, the upper part of the cabin glazing is raised at an accentuated angle leading towards a high top turret (B2-*Stand*), while the rear gun position (B1-*Stand*) sits in more sharply angled glazing. The mock forward and rear armament represent MG 81Zs (*EN Archive*)

In this mock-up design there is no B2-*Stand* gun turret and the rear canopy is aerodynamically smoother. Note the extensive view forward from the pilot's position and minimal hindrance from instrumentation (*EN Archive*)

that of the original Ju 85 concept in order to recognise up-to-date tactical and technical requirements. It bore some similarities to the features of the test cockpit of the Ju 88 V5 from which the ill-fated Ju 288 project took influence.

Ultimately, a run of ten prototypes, or more accurately 'experimental' aircraft, ensued, all assigned *Versuchs* (test) numbers. The first, built at Dessau, was Ju 88 V23 Wk-Nr 7023 D-ARYB (NK+AO), which was based on the fuselage and main components of a Ju 88A-5. Impressively, this machine took to the air for the first time on 19 June 1940. The aircraft was fitted with 1100-hp Jumo 211B engines, and it was judged favourably. The V23 was designated a bomber, and it was to have additional ETC bomb racks fitted outboard of the engines. Wk-Nr 7023 would be refitted with BMW 801 engines.

Three more prototypes were completed at Dessau by late 1940, these aircraft being configured in line with planned usage of the B series and trialled with BMW 801 and Jumo 211B engines at both Junkers and the *Erprobungsstelle* Rechlin. V24 Wk-Nr 024 D-ASGQ (NK+AL) completed its first flight on 30 July 1940 and V25 Wk-Nr 025(?) (NK+AK) flew for the first time on 26 September 1940. V26 Wk-Nr 026 (NK+AL) comprised an A-1 airframe to which was fitted the new cockpit section and two 1600 hp BMW 801MA 14-cylinder radial engines. This powerplant was the successor to the BMW 139, with the Jumo 213 still being unavailable as a result of production problems at Junkers' engine plant.

The V26 flew for the first time towards the end of 1940, and although its performance just edged that of the Ju 88A-1, the RLM did not view this as justification for disruption to production of the A series. In any case, these aircraft were viewed as being part of the *overall* Ju 88 development programme, rather than as an initiative towards an entirely new type of aircraft.

In many ways this was fortuitous, because despite Junkers' initial optimism over the new cockpit, testing revealed that it was still restrictive in size on account of the fact that it could not accommodate three manned gun positions, unlike the Ju 88A-5 in which spatial problems were to be solved by widening the canopy (in essence, 'bulging' it). Additionally, the Jumo 211 offered little real increase in performance over the A-5, which pointed to the BMW 801 as the required engine, but again, availability was limited.

The Dessau design and engineering team went back to the drawing board, and in the autumn of 1940 work commenced on a second batch of *Versuchs* machines that featured an enhanced cockpit design and an increase in overall size. The first example to roll out was Ju 88 V27 Wk-Nr 7027 D-AWLN, which took to the air on 27 December 1940. The V27 also had a larger, lengthened cockpit, something that was accomplished by extending the cabin area by 700 mm between the pilot and radio operator positions. This allowed the fitment of a manned, powered dorsal turret armed with 13 mm MG 131 machine gun and 7.9 mm MG 81Z (*Zwilling* – 'twin') machine gun sets in the nose and rear cockpit positions. Balance was maintained by weights to the tail. Ju 88 V28 Wk-Nr 7028, followed in December 1940, with V29 Wk-Nr 7029 taking to the air for the first time on 21 January 1941, although this machine would be lost in an accident on 6 July of that year.

It is possible that at this point, three basic sub-variants were proposed somewhere within the RLM system for what would become, officially, the Ju 88B series – the B-1 as a level- and dive-bomber, the B-2 as a two-seat reconnaissance aircraft and the B-3 possibly as a two-seat *Zerstörer,* although this is not clear. However, connecting specific *Versuchs* aircraft with specific operational roles is difficult. Furthermore, if the B is seen as a new or enhanced series variant of the A *Schnellbomber* and the subsequent purpose-built Ju 88C as a *Zerstörer* and the Ju 88D as a long-range photo-reconnaissance aircraft (based on the Ju 88A-4/A-5), respectively, there was not, in theory, the need for reconnaissance or *Zerstörer* sub-variants in the B-series. Nevertheless, some sources maintain that one prototype was tested as such, albeit temporarily, at Rechlin.

These later machines were based on the A-4 but had the lengthened wings of the A-5, which had extended outer wing panels, inset metal-skinned ailerons and more angular wingtips, as designed for the A-4, taking the span to 20.08 m. The fuselage was also lengthened by 70 cm to improve stability, resulting in an overall length of 14.45 m. The pre-production B-0 was to be armed with three 7.9 mm MG 81Z machine gun sets in nose (A-*Stand*), dorsal (B-*Stand*) and ventral (C-*Stand*) positions (although armament configurations would be inconsistent), and it would carry a maximum bomb payload of 2500 kg. The majority were built as unarmed reconnaissance aircraft, however.

Ultimately, the B series never progressed into full production. Indeed, there seems to have been an inexplicable reversal in RLM decision-making, which, in 1940, initially favoured full-scale series production of the B, if possible in early 1941. This had been halted by late 1940. One hypothesis for the latter decision was that abandoning the B series would allow further development of a new reconnaissance variant which would take advantage of BMW engines able to offer higher speed at greater altitude.

A number of what were termed B-0s were eventually delivered to the *Aufklärungsgruppe der Oberbefehlshaber der Luftwaffe* (Aufkl.Gr. Ob.d.L. – Reconnaissance Group of the Luftwaffe High Command), where they joined Jumo-engined V24 D-ASGQ. This aircraft had undergone testing at Rechlin prior to being delivered to the unit.

Throughout the summer of 1941, the V25, and probably the V26, V28 and V29 (the latter two fitted with BMW 801 engines), underwent conversion to reconnaissance configuration. This meant the aircraft were not fitted with a bombsight, outer wing racks and dive brakes, and the bomb-bay was faired over so as to accommodate a large fuel tank and three cameras, the latter operating through two windows on the starboard side and one on the port side. The B-0 was capable of a top speed of between 500–540 km/h, had a range of 2850 km and a ceiling of 9400 m.

Alongside Ju 86Ps, the aircraft were used by the *Versuchsstelle für Höhenflüge* of the Aufkl.Gr. d.Ob.d.L., under Major Theodor Rowehl,

The Ju 88B-0, possibly K9+RH, flown by Oberleutnant Cornelius Noell of the Aufkl.Gr. Ob.d.L. on long-range photographic reconnaissance flights over the Soviet Union in June 1941. It was powered by BMW 801 engines and carried minimal armament on account of what was considered the aircraft's superior speed and operational altitudes (*EN Archive*)

to carry out long-range, high-altitude photographic mapping missions over western Russia ahead of the planned invasion of the Soviet Union. Some sources maintain that these missions were flown with either lightly armed or even unarmed aircraft. Unfortunately, the V24, as K9+QH, was shot down and destroyed on 1 September 1941 while assigned to 1.(F)/Aufkl.Gr. Ob.d.L.

But if the Ju 88B-0 needed any testimony to its capabilities, this came on 22 October 1941 when Oberleutnant Cornelius Noell and Leutnant Josef Bisping of 1.(F)/Aufkl.Gr. Ob.d.L were both awarded the Knight's Cross following a mission they had flown on 26 June, four days after the commencement of Operation *Barbarossa*. They had taken off in their Ju 88B-0 from a forward Luftwaffe fighter airfield and flown as far as Moscow, where, ignoring both Soviet anti-aircraft fire and enemy fighters that proved unable to catch the Junkers, they photographed enemy airfields around the capital city whilst using its broadcasting station as a homing beacon.

In another example of the B-0's range capability, in September 1942 Major Siegfried Knemeyer, another highly accomplished pilot with the Aufkl.Gr. Ob.d.L., flew the type on reconnaissance flights from Balcic, in Bulgaria, as far as Baku on the Caspian Sea. 'To get there', Knemeyer recalled, 'I flew in a Ju 88B, with full-vision cockpit and BMW 801s, south over the north coast of Turkey, past Mount Ararat, to the Caspian Sea and the Caucasus. I flew four operations from Balcic to Baku. The Russians had no fighters with mechanical superchargers. Their performance dropped off above 4500 m. Others who tried it from Nikolayev [in the southern Ukraine] didn't make it back'.

In broad terms, the Ju 88B was viewed favourably by the crews of the Aufkl.Gr. Ob.d.L.. Exactly how much influence Rowehl had is not certain, suffice to say Junkers Dessau embarked on building three more *Versuchs* machines – the V30 to V32 – using components and tooling that were still available. The first aircraft, V30 Wk-Nr 7030 D-AFAG, was completed in November 1941 with BMW engines, followed by V31 Wk-Nr 7030, also with BMWs, and the last, V32 Wk-Nr 7032, rolling out in January 1942 fitted with Jumo 213A engines, at least for a period. These aircraft lacked a dorsal turret (which refined the cockpit aerodynamically), but incorporated a number of internal revisions and improvements.

Those aircraft retained by Junkers were used for testing purposes both at the factory and at Rechlin for the RLM's programme to replace the increasingly out-dated Ju 88A bomber. With the B series effectively abandoned, and the C and D designations assigned to progressive and purpose-built fighter and reconnaissance variants of the Ju 88, the suffix 'E' was applied to the new programme.

In an independent factory initiative at Dessau, from May 1941 V27 Wk-Nr 7027 D-AWLN was re-fitted with BMW 801C engines and a powered dorsal turret armed with a single 13 mm MG 131 machine gun which supplemented a new nose-mounted 20 mm MG 151 cannon (replacing the MG 81Z) and machine gun in the rear cockpit. Included in a range of modifications, the radio equipment was also upgraded. In this configuration, the aircraft was designated the V27/1.

Work proceeded slowly, and the next aircraft to be configured as an 'E'-programme prototype was the Ju 88 V30, which became the Ju 88 V30/1 in the spring of 1942. This was followed later the same year by three more aircraft manufactured at Junkers' Bernburg plant – the BMW 801-powered V61 Wk-Nr 160051(?) DE+EV, V62 DE+EW and V63 Wk-Nr 140699(?) CE+XA, with in-line Jumo 211s, although these were subsequently replaced by new Jumo 213As (when it became the V63/1). With the fitment of a turret equipped with an MG 151, they were used for testing purposes for what would emerge as the Ju 188A.

No production of the E-0 ensued at this stage, but disappointment on the part of the RLM with another project meant that the aircraft had not seen the end of its days. In July 1939 the RLM's *Technisches Amt* issued a specification requirement to Junkers, Arado, Dornier and Focke-Wulf for a replacement of the He 111 and Ju 88 under the project name 'Bomber B'. The Ministry's requirement was for a 'next generation' aircraft to be powered by twin 2000 hp Jumo 222 engines, which were still under development, 'capable of striking targets anywhere within the British Isles with a 4000-kg bombload at a maximum speed of 600 km/h'. Furthermore, the aircraft was to carry a crew of three or four in a pressurised cabin protected by armament housed in remotely controlled turrets.

Junkers, at some advantage as a result of its work on the Ju 88, was ordered by the RLM to move with urgency, but not to submit any proposal which was a major reworking of the Ju 88. The company's submission was the Ju 288, an aircraft which the RLM hoped would replace the Ju 88 from late 1943.

However, development and progress with the Ju 288 proceeded slowly and suffered from delays, but in the meantime Junkers had continued to work independently on what was now at least referred to as the Ju 88E-0. In September 1941 the V27, as CG+NC, was fitted with two 1600 hp BMW 801MA radials and wings designed with even more pointed tips, increasing the span by another two metres. Despite the bomber's EDL 131 dorsal turret, the basic rear airframe shape still resembled the Ju 88A.

Eventually, in October 1942, with continuing delays to the Ju 288 and the prospect of that aircraft not being available in 1943, the RLM officially authorised work to continue on the Ju 88E. In a bizarre example of RLM planning, an order had been placed for no fewer than 430 Ju 88 'E-1s' engineered for tropical operations. Nevertheless, this contributed to the speeding up of the development programme, with the Ju 88E continuing to be seen as the successor to the Ju 88A bomber.

However, paradoxically, and in parallel, another short run of *Versuchs* aircraft, considered as set apart from the E-variant test programme, was built in an effort to cure the issues of weight and horizontal stability in the Junkers. Firstly, the Ju 88 V41 Wk-Nr 5002 D-AFBY (DE+KD) appeared, fitted with BMW 801 engines. It flew in late 1941. The V41 was followed by V43 Wk-Nr 1530 D-AFBK (RF+IQ), similarly powered by BMW engines, and then the Ju 88 V44 Wk-Nr 1687 NF+KQ. Both examples also first flew in late 1941.

In attempting to overcome the aforementioned weight and stability issues, not only were the Junkers engineers successful, they had also produced aircraft that possessed greatly improved in-flight handling, manoeuvrability and performance. This was timely, for pressure to find a suitable bomber replacement was coming from on high. On 18 March 1943, Reichsmarschall Göring chaired a conference at his country estate at Karinhall on problems related to aircraft production. It was a sombre event, and an irritated Göring, who was looking for suitable aircraft with which to bomb Britain, lamented;

'Even the Ju 88 is an aircraft which was thoroughly up to standard in the first years of the war and which today can only just be used at night for operations against Britain on rare occasions when conditions are especially favourable. I might well say that I have witnessed one reverse after the other – crises of almost catastrophic proportions.'

'However, the situation as regards engines appears if anything to be even worse. Once again there has been one promise after another, but comparatively few have been kept. To take just one example – by the time the 801 had been developed after extensive operational experience to the point at which it was comparatively serviceable and would outlast several operations without needing to be changed, the enemy had already gone far ahead in terms of horsepower. Thus, just when the engine was at last beginning to become fit for operational employment, it had once again already been long outclassed.'

At the same conference, Göring lumped the prospective Ju 188 in with the He 177 as an aircraft that was not reliable enough to reach even Glasgow as a bombing target.

An underside view of Ju 88 V44 NF+KQ, photographed while on a test flight and showing the unarmed *Bodenwanne* and ETC bomb racks fitted to the inner wings. The aircraft was also fitted with tufts on its outer wing uppersurfaces to assess aerodynamic forces (*EN Archive*)

It would be the Ju 88 V44, the most advanced of the three *Versuchs* machines, and completed with a larger and squarer vertical tail and rudder assembly intended to counter the instability problems, that emerged as the first aircraft built with the shape of what was to be the Ju 188. The V44, which first flew on 24 June 1942, offered salvation to the RLM in its search for a next-generation bomber in the face of the failure of the Ju 288 and the quickly ageing Ju 88A. The ministry thus wiped the slate clean. No longer was the programme to continue under the 'Ju 88E' variant designation, but rather, from

The fuselage of this Ju 88B, on jacks, appears to have suffered some damage, suggesting it is undergoing repair. Note that the entire central and rear sections of the cockpit glazing have been removed. Due to the absence of a forward-firing weapon, the aircraft would appear to be a reconnaissance variant, possibly one serving with the Aufkl.Gr. Ob.d.L. in 1941–42 (*EN Archive*)

August 1942, an entirely new model was to be created known as the Ju 188, and the V44 was to become the recognised prototype for the new type as the Ju 188 V1 and a new Ju 188E series.

A second prototype, V2 Wk-Nr 260151, was built at Junkers' Bernburg plant and joined the test programme in January 1943. At around the same time, plans were put in place for series production at Bernburg, with aircraft being able to take either BMW 801 or Jumo 213 inline engines.

With the faith of the RLM behind the new design, impetus started to gather, and work on a new *Erkunder* (reconnaissance) version, the F-1, commenced. Wk-Nr 10016 had a GM-1 nitrous oxide boost installation and commenced flight-testing from the *Erprobungsstelle* at Rechlin in August.

The first examples of the Ju 188E-0 were rolled out from Bernburg in February 1943, the run featuring both types of engine, followed quickly in April by the E-1 designed to accommodate pilot, navigator/bomb-aimer, radio operator and gunner, and powered by 1600-hp BMW 801ML units. The E-0s were mainly fitted with BMW engines, while those machines powered by the Jumo were designated Ju 188A-0s. The E variant was fitted with dive brakes for dive-bombing, while the A was planned as a level bomber. The former preceded the latter in its introduction to operations.

The E-0 run featured assessment installations of radios and antennas, and two aircraft were also known to have been used for special armament testing. Standard armament for the E and F series comprised a nose-mounted MG 151 in the A-*Stand*, an MG 131 in the B1- and B2-*Stands* and an MG 81Z in the C-*Stand*. Testing with the E-1 specification had concluded in September 1942.

Concurrent with this activity, the Ju 88 V63/1 fitted with Jumo 213A engines continued testing, being moved over to the Ju 188 programme in the autumn of 1942. The Ju 188 (F-1 *trop*, A-2 and D-2 *trop*) was included with types contained in *Lieferplan* (production schedule) 223 of April 1943 for late 1943/early 1944. Three Ju 188A-0s were completed in the summer of 1943, and although it may have been the intention to fit these with Jumo engines, ongoing delays with their delivery resulted in postponement of the planned Jumo 213-powered bomber (A-0) and reconnaissance aircraft (D-0), as well as the proposed C/D bomber and reconnaissance variants with MG 131Z tail armament.

CHAPTER TWO

ENTER THE 'E'

The shape of the new Ju 188 emerges. This somewhat worn-looking aircraft is an early Ju 188E-0 with a tall antenna mast (*EN Archive*)

The first Ju 188 variant to be evaluated meaningfully for operational service by the Luftwaffe was the E-1, examples of which were delivered from Junkers in the summer of 1943. Production was consistent but low-volume, with December 1943 seeing the highest monthly output at 63 E- and F-models. By the end of the year, a total of 283 E- and F-models had been built.

The company had issued a duel *Baubeschreibung* (build description/outline) in January 1943 for the E-1, a variant described as a *Kampfflugzeug* (standard bomber with, in theory, diving-bombing capability) and the F-1 *Fernerkunder* (long-range reconnaissance variant). By September, the RLM had issued its handbook for the E-1.

The aircraft, powered by BMW 801 radial engines (using the 1600 hp ML or 1700 hp D or G-2 versions), was 15.03 m in length and had a wingspan of 22 m. Its height from ground level to the top of the B2-*Stand* was 4.45 m and, from the tailwheel at ground level to the top of the tail fin, 3.57 m. The clearance between the main wheels was 5.77 m. The main structural components of the aircraft, which were designed to be removed and replaced with relative ease, were the wings, engine units, landing flaps, ailerons, main- and tailwheels, tail fin, rudder and horizontal stabilisers.

The crew of four entered the aircraft via a ladder and hatch beneath the rear of the forward fuselage and climbed up into the cockpit area with its bulbous canopy. In reality, despite the amount of glazing, the view from the cockpit was hampered by the multi-panelled framework, and vision was impaired to some extent by the lower quality of glass being manufactured at this stage within wartime Germany.

The glazing frame was built with an integrated, rubberised gun mount for the nose weapon fitted on the lower front starboard side, directly above which was a solid panel for protection, while on the panels above that (and on the corresponding panels to port) the glass was marked with coloured inclined lines for diving flight – the aircraft was fitted with dive brakes. Externally, beneath the nose gun mount, a sharp steel cutter – or *Kuto-Nase* – could be fitted to sever barrage balloon cables. Below the *Kuto-Nase*, as the nosed curved down towards the *Bodenwanne* (ventral bulge/gondola), there was a Nordland heated pane that could be controlled from a switch on the port side cockpit wall panel in the pilot's position.

The bomb-aimer/gunner had a rear-view mirror fitted to the glazing frame above his position, and the cockpit also benefited from anti-glare curtains to the front and rear. Directly above the pilot's seat was an emergency exit hatch. The turning frame of the B2-*Stand* fitting was located immediately behind the hatch, and it was lined with cushioned padding. There were also sliding window panels on either side of the cockpit for both ventilation and external communication.

Armoured panels were set into the upper framework behind the B1-*Stand* and in the lower frame running around the B1-*Stand*, above which the whole canopy was detachable through the use of an ejector handle fitted on the rear starboard side framework. When the canopy detached, the side panels were also loosened. There was also a night vision window panel.

The pilot sat in a centrally positioned, adjustable armoured steel seat with an armoured head protector, arm rests and shoulder and waist straps. In front of him was a height-adjustable control column, on top of which the steering control yoke could be moved transversely. The yoke, inset with a clock, had the bomb release button on its left grip and, on the right, the auto-pilot controls, armament uncocking button, elevator trim tab switch and the button for the FuG 16 radio. Further back from the pilot were the emergency switch and pump for oil pressure. The rudder and brakes were activated through foot pumps.

Looking directly ahead, the pilot would see the emergency rate-of-turn indicator fitted to the upper curve of the cockpit framework, below which was a vertically aligned panel containing gauges for the radio

The steering column horn in a Ju 188 transversed to the right. A clock is inset in the centre of the horn. On the left grip is the bomb release button, while the right grip included the armament uncocking and FuG 16 radio buttons. Ahead, fitted to the glazing framework, is a panel which included airspeed and rate-of-climb indicators and an artificial horizon (*EN Archive*)

The forward part of the pilot's control console in a Ju 188E, located to his left. Ahead of the throttle levers is the lamp indicator panel, while to the side is the brake for the power selector lever. On the raised panel are the magneto switches at right, and below these the dive switch with trim and dive brake control. To the left are the controls for the landing flaps and tail mechanism, switches for automatic propeller control and the gauges for the trim indicator, double tachometer and double boost pressure meter (*EN Archive*)

navigation indicator, airspeed and rate-of-climb indicators, artificial horizon and AFN 101 indicator for the FuG 101 altimeter.

Beside him to the left was a console with the throttle levers, magneto levers, engine fuel cut-off lever, landing gear switch, landing flaps and horizontal stabiliser control switches, dive switch, double tachometer and radiator louvre adjustment controls. Additionally, there were handwheels for trimming and a small 12-lamp panel with position indicators for dive brakes, landing flaps and stabilisers. There were also gauges and dials for the bank indicator, rev counter, supercharging pressure indicator, oxygen flow sensor and pressure indicator. On the cockpit wall above was a switch panel, intercom connector socket and oxygen system tube.

From November 1944, Oberleutnant Peter Stahl flew the Ju 188 with *Kommando Olga*, a detachment of I./KG 200 (see Chapter Four). Although he saw action in the later Jumo-engined A-model, the recollections in his post-war memoirs offer a good assessment of the aircraft from the pilot's perspective;

'On entering the aircraft, an old Ju 88 hand was immediately struck by the completely altered forward cabin. The fully glazed nose section was of streamlined shape, without the "step" below the pilot's windscreen. This configuration gave an unobstructed view forward and continued almost vertically downwards. As on the Ju 88, there was an electrically heated Plexiglas panel fitted in the floor between the rudder pedals so that the pilot could have a good view underneath as well.

'The layout of the instruments and various control levers differed completely from the Ju 88 – the pilot's vision was no longer obstructed by instrument panels or other fittings. An instrument panel with the most essential navigational instruments was attached against the cabin roof to the right of centre. All other instruments and devices were fitted in special panels alongside the port and starboard walls of the cabin.

'I found the advanced layout of the pilot's seat and controls a real boon compared to that of the Ju 88. Coming in for landing in the previous model [Ju 88], I first had to loosen my harness straps to be able to reach all the necessary levers on the long instrument panel with my left hand. Not any more: on the Ju 188 the whole procedure was made easy by a set of switches and press-buttons at a handy distance around the seat. For instance, trimming of the elevators, which regulated the landing speed and gliding angle, was done by just one switch on the control column horn. It was no longer necessary to turn a hand-wheel somewhere on the cabin wall.

'All indicators and visual displays for the positions of the undercarriage, landing flaps, trim and propeller pitch were concentrated in one single multi-display instrument that conveyed the information either by means of light signals or symbols. Thanks to this, the pilot was informed at a glance of the momentary situation of the aircraft, and had almost unlimited time to concentrate on landing and what went on around him.'

The bomb-aimer had a fold-down seat and would use a knee cushion for aiming, and there were viewing windows looking forward and to the rear. The glazed nose also housed the *Lotfernrohr* (*Lotfe*) 7D optical bombsight, which was the latest version of the *Lotfernrohr* sight manufactured by Carl Zeiss. A *Stuvi* (*Sturzkampfvisier*) dive-bombing sight could also be installed next to the vertically aligned instrument panel in front of the pilot. To the left, facing forward, this position had access to the lever for the blind-landing device, emergency rudder control and an emergency compass. To the right were the bomb levers and the bomb-aimer's folding seat. The bomb-aimer would also connect up a support belt to a catch on the wall above the seat, next to which was his oxygen system connection point.

To the right side of the cockpit were three groups of switches, buttons and gauges. Firstly, at what would have been just about knee height, was the armament panel switch box, then the bomb-drop control and a fuse board. Directly above was a line of controls containing the bomb fuse arming switch box, the bomb-drop sequence setting switch and FuG 16 controls. Above this group were the oil temperature indicators, a four-way

Schematic taken from the Ju 188E/F *Baubeschreibung* of January 1943 showing the internal layout of the cockpit looking from the starboard side to the port side wall and internal access to the Bodenwanne (*EN Archive*)

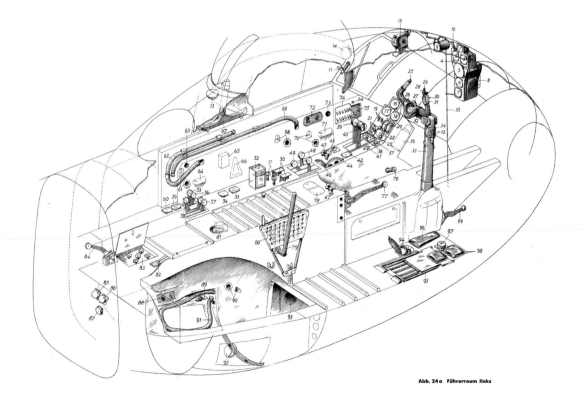

Abb. 24a Führerraum links

oil and fuel cut-off valve, outside air temperature indicator, gyro switch, *Peil* radio direction finder switch, airspeed sensor, altimeter indicator and corrector panel.

To the right of these was a panel holding the indicators and sensors for the individual crewmembers' oxygen flow and pressure. A flare signal pistol could be inserted into a dedicated stowage socket by its barrel for easy use. Aft, towards the radio operator's seat, was the emergency hydraulic pump lever, a master switch panel and the dinghy release handle. Manual fuel pump levers were also located here.

The radio operator's adjustable seat was positioned behind the pilot's, facing out through the B1-*Stand* and installed above Frames 6 and 7. To his right, as he sat, was an inset panel with the oxygen cylinder valve knobs and a release lever for a drop tank if carried. Between the pilot's and radio operator's seats was an emergency oil pump lever.

There was a leather 'emergency seat' with waist straps and a footrest provided for a gunner to the left of the radio operator's position facing aft.

A folding support aided entry and exit to/from the ventral armoured *Bodenwanne* ('gondola'). Head armour was provided for the gunner and more armour covered the hydraulics oil tank. The rear of the gondola contained an emergency release handle, protected by a safety button, which could jettison the armoured crew entrance hatch.

In the case of the E-1 bomber, the bomb compartment between Frames 9 and 15 was covered by four doors that were operated by an electric motor activated by a toggle switch in the bomb-aimer's area of the cockpit. An emergency release rod system could be used if necessary for the main internal and external wing loads.

An overview of bombload configurations for the Ju 188E-1, with options for 70, 250, 500, 1000 and 1800 kg bombs, as well as aerial mines. To the top left of the drawing are listed the various types of underwing carriers and racks (*EN Archive*)

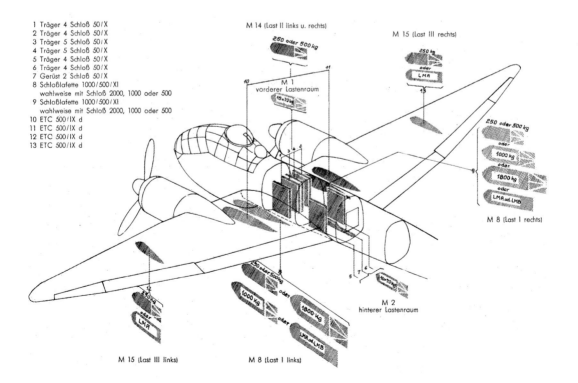

1 Träger 4 Schloß 50 / X
2 Träger 4 Schloß 50 / X
3 Träger 5 Schloß 50 / X
4 Träger 5 Schloß 50 / X
5 Träger 5 Schloß 50 / X
6 Träger 4 Schloß 50 / X
7 Gerüst 2 Schloß 50 / X
8 Schloßlafette 1000 / 500 / XI
  wahlweise mit Schloß 2000, 1000 oder 500
9 Schloßlafette 1000 / 500 / XI
  wahlweise mit Schloß 2000, 1000 oder 500
10 ETC 500 / IX d
11 ETC 500 / IX d
12 ETC 500 / IX d
13 ETC 500 / IX d

M 14 (Last II links u. rechts)
M 15 (Last III rechts)
250 oder 500 kg
250 kg
oder
LMA
M 1
vorderer Lastenraum
15 × 70 kg
250 oder 500 kg
oder
1000 kg
oder
1800 kg
oder
LMA od. LMB
M 8 (Last I rechts)
250 oder 500 kg
oder
1000 kg
oder
1800 kg
oder
LMA od. LMB
15 × 70 kg
M 2
hinterer Lastenraum
250 kg
oder
LMA
M 15 (Last III links)
M 8 (Last I links)

One feature of the Ju 188E-1 was its flexible and wide-ranging ordnance load capability. In the *Rüstsatz* M1/M2 configuration, a total of 1960 kg could be accommodated, with 18 70-kg bombs carried in the forward bomb-bay from *Schloß* 50/X carriers in a 4-5-5-4 alignment across the bay, and another ten such bombs in a 4-2-4 alignment in the rear bay, the centre two being suspended from a bar.

In the *Rüstsatz* M8 configuration, up to 3600 kg could be carried using either 250- or 500-kg bombs, 1000- or 1800-kg bombs or 500-kg *Luftminenbombe A* (LMA – parachute air mine) or 1000-kg *Luftminenbombe B* (LMB) in each of the left and right sides of the bomb-bay and fitted to *Schloßlafette* 1000/500/XI 500 and/or *Schloß* 500, 1000 or 2000 carriers. Externally, two 250-kg bombs or one 500-kg bomb could be carried on ETC 500/IXd underwing racks inboard of the engines in the M14 configuration, while a further 250-kg bomb or an LMA could be carried on ETC 500/IXd racks under each outer wing in the M15 configuration.

Fuel was contained in a 415-litre inner wing tank and a 425-litre outer-wing tank in each wing, with oil tanks behind each engine and an auxiliary oil tank in the outer wing. The associated oil pressure and control gauges were located on the starboard side instrument panel in the cockpit.

A 900-litre under-wing jettisonable auxiliary tank could be carried below the location of the inner wing tanks. Further *Rüstsatz* fuel options were available for long-range bombing and reconnaissance operations, with the *Rüstsatz* B 1 allowed for the fitment of a 1220-litre tank in the fuselage between Frames 9 and 12, while with the B 2 option, a second tank of 680 litres capacity could be installed behind, between Frames 12 and 15. A rapid discharge pipe was fitted running aft through the fuselage to vent out beneath the tail assembly.

Defensive armament comprised one flexibly mounted, belt-fed 20 mm Mauser MG 151/20 cannon in the glazed nose (A-*Stand*). The weapon was held in a *Lafette* L151/3 mount, which could be locked for rigid firing, and had an electrically operated triggering system. It was sighted by means of an externally mounted ring-and-bead sight. Ammunition was stowed in a semi-circular container that moulded into the curvature of the lower cockpit. Spent shell cases were ejected via a flexible hose chute through a port in the starboard lower forward fuselage. The gun could be secured to a lashing point on the starboard side of the canopy.

The B1-*Stand* (rear cockpit – dorsal) was armed with a 13 mm belt-fed Rheinmetall-Borsig MG 131 machine gun firing through a *Panzerglas* (armoured glass) circular panel. Like the MG 151, it was sighted using an externally mounted ring-and-bead sight. The gun could be secured to a lashing point on the upper framework of the canopy. Ammunition was stored in two containers, one mounted to each side wall of the aircraft, and was fed to the gun using a caster-operated feed. Spent shell cases were ejected via a flexible hose chute through a port in the starboard side of the *Bodenwanne*. The B1-*Stand* was protected by panels of armour around the tops of Frames 8a and 9.

A further MG 131 could be fitted in the low-profile, powered dome of the B2-*Stand*. The gun was held in place by an armoured shield, and

The B2-*Stand* gun dome fitted with a 13 mm MG 131 machine gun. Note the anti-glare curtains on the inside of the panels below and the rim of the second gun mount visible to right (*EN Archive*)

it could be secured to a lashing point on the small dome control panel located in the well. The weapon was aimed by a *Revi* (reflector) sight. After firing, spent cases were discharged downwards through a flexible hose chute into a leather pouch. The gunner sat on a small leather cushion and was enclosed by a metal backrest and frame. He pulled himself up to operate the gun with the aid of a hand grip located on the bottom of the well rim. He controlled rotation of the dome by means of a drive handle located on the rim of the dome well. There was also a manual overdrive, and a release lever to jettison the dome in an emergency. The dome also featured a small air vent.

The rear-firing, ventral C-*Stand* position featured a 7.9 mm MG 81Z twin machine gun set installed in a jettisonable glazed framework protected by armoured side panels at the aft end of the *Bodenwanne*. The gun was fitted to a flexible mount, and it could be secured by suspending the rear of the weapon from a leather strap. The gunner would lie prone to operate the weapons, and he was protected by an armoured panel. Ammunition was fed by two bracketed chutes from twin containers fitted to the bulkhead wall at Frame 8a. Spent shells were ejected through a port in the floor of the *Bodenwanne*.

The boxes containing the converters for the FuG 10P long and short wave transceiver used for R/T and W/T, the FuBl 2 F blind-landing system and the FuG 16 VHF transceiver, as well as the adjustment control for the FuG 16, were fitted to a panel on the inner starboard wall of the rear fuselage forward of the tail assembly. They shared this space with a relay box, distributor, resistance box, transmitter/receiver and sounder for the FuG 25 system.

The Ju 188E-2 was similar to the E-1 but was intended as a torpedo-bomber. It duly carried FuG 200 *Hohentwiel* ship-search radar and lacked a dorsal turret and dive-bombing equipment. When installed, the FuG 200 was able to cover a radius of about 100 kilometres, weather permitting. Intended to replace the *Rostock Gerät* search equipment from the summer of 1943, and developed and manufactured by C. Lorenz AG of Berlin, the FuG 200 was a low-UHF band system that had a greater range (60–80 kilometres) than its predecessor when used to locate individual ships. FuG 200 also had less impact on aircraft speed because of its small antenna array.

Externally, the transmitter antenna for the FuG 200 comprised eight end-fed, half-wave horizontal dipoles arranged in colinear pairs mounted on brackets in the nose of an aircraft, facing forward in the line of flight.

The receiver had no r-f amplification, but was connected, by means of a motor-driven switch, alternately to two antennas fitted on the right and left sides of the fuselage at angles of 30 degrees to the line of flight. Internally, the apparatus was powered by a motor generator and consisted of a transmitter and modulator, an indicator unit (the *Sichtgerät* [SG] 200) and a control or switch box (*Schaltkasten* [SK] 200). There was a two-tube, high-power transmitter, a superheterodyne receiver and a cathode ray tube (CRT) indicator.

The switch box, fitted with four knobs, was located in the observer's position in the aircraft. The top left knob controlled the zero point, the top right knob controlled the focus of the trace, the bottom left knob changed the range from 0 to 150 kilometres for search and navigational aid for approach and attack, and, finally, the bottom right knob governed the brightness of the trace. A two-way switch at the top of the box turned the equipment on and off, while the lowermost knob remotely controlled the gain in the receiver. A lever to the right of the unit was self-centring and made a slight adjustment in the frequency. A left-hand switch was used when the *Hohentwiel* was being employed at altitudes in excess of 2000 m.

The range scale etched on the glass of the CRT screen coincided with the vertical time base, and was calibrated from zero to 150 kilometres at ten-kilometre intervals – the distance between the ten-kilometre marks was progressively smaller as extreme range was reached. The vertical time base took the form of a screen with 15 parallel horizontal lines reading 0 to 150 kilometres (from bottom to top). Because of ground returns, satisfactory readings could not be obtained at less than three kilometres. To offset that, some FuG 200 sets were fitted with a switch which magnified scale so that close ranges could be read off to the nearest 50 m. The device operated on a frequency range of 570 megacycles and had a pulse recurrence frequency of 600 cycles per second.

As well as the FuG 200, the Ju 188E-2 and F reconnaissance variants could be installed with FuG 217R *Neptun* tail warning equipment, although it is likely that only a relatively small number of aircraft benefited from this.

The Ju 188E-2 could be fitted with two 765-kg LT F5b torpedoes under the wings between the engines and the fuselage, or an internal bomb-load of 3000 kg.

The Ju 188E/F could also be fitted out for tropical operations, incorporating dust filters and other fitments to protect sensitive equipment and minimise damage that could be expected from tropical conditions. For the crew, there was provision for two- and five-litre water bottles, a machine pistol and an axe, all stowed in the cockpit. An emergency transmitter was installed into the fuselage at Frame 15, a water filter at Frame 18 and distress flares, antenna equipment, a rubber mattress and a further 8.5-litre water canister between Frames 20 and 24. However, few, if any, such tropical variants were completed to such a specification.

Having flown DF+EW, Fliegerstabsingeneur Hans-Werner Lerche, a test pilot at the *Erprobungsstelle* Rechlin, felt that the Ju 188 was 'a fast and very manoeuvrable bomber'. It remained to be seen how effective it would be in that role.

CHAPTER THREE

SERVICE DEBUT

A Jumo 213-engined Ju 188A possibly of KG 6, whose aircraft were known to have double-ringed spinners. The bomber carries an MG 151 in the A-*Stand* position, and it is fitted with flame dampers and a '*Kuto-Nase*' cutting frame. Note the ladder leaning against the open access hatch (*Hermann*)

To test and evaluate the Ju 188E-1 for operational service and to familiarise instructors and technical specialists on the type who would then assist with its smooth introduction into operational units, on 1 March 1943 the Luftwaffe established *Erprobungsstaffel Ju 188* under Major Helmut Schmid. The unit, which would have operating elements at Rechlin and Vannes, in western France, soon became known more formally as the *Erprobungskommando der Luftwaffe (E.Kdo der Lw.) 188*. That there was a need for the unit at all is perhaps best encapsulated in the view of Ju 188 pilot Oberleutnant Peter Stahl;

'In the Ju 188 we had an aircraft that differed in so many technical details and its flying performance from all other comparable machines, that its safe and successful operational use depended completely on how familiar the pilot and his crew were with it.'

The *Kommando* was formed from selected military and civilian personnel drawn from the *Erprobungsstelle* and Junkers, together with bomber crews from KG 6. At the end of July, it is believed the *Staffel* relocated to Chièvres, to the southwest of Brussels.

In August 1943, *Erprobungsstaffel Ju 188*, by this time comprising only the personnel from KG 6, together with personnel from the disbanded 2.(*Ausb. u. Erp.*)/KG 60, were used to form a new 4./KG 66 at Avord, in France, which was to be equipped with Ju 188s. I./KG 60 had had some early experience with the Ju 188 since, according to information gleaned by the Allies from captured German aircrew, one example had been delivered to the unit for assessment in 1942 (probably a Ju 88B) when the *Gruppe* was based at Tours, in France, under the ultimate command of Major Dietrich Peltz.

In March 1941, Peltz, who had flown both Ju 87s and Ju 88s, had been appointed to command II./KG 77, and by 12 July that year he had flown his 200th combat mission. After an impressive operational record, in which he served over Poland, France, the British Isles and the Soviet Union, Peltz had been awarded the Swords to the Knight's Cross with Oakleaves on 23 July 1943, having undertaken around 320 missions as a Stuka and bomber pilot. In January 1942, he took command of the *Verbandsführerschule für Kampfflieger* (Bomber Unit Leaders' School) at Foggia, in Italy, which later moved to Tours. In August 1942, this school was redesignated I./KG 60 as an anti-shipping unit, with Peltz as its *Kommandeur*.

Peltz had been convinced of the efficacy of formation dive-bombing

Watched by an aircrew officer, groundcrew of an unidentified unit enjoy a lighter moment using a Ju 188E or F as a prop (*Carrick*)

with Ju 88s, which, he claimed, combined the accuracy of Ju 87 dive-bombing with the effect of pattern bombing, while at the same time giving the Ju 88 material protection against fighter attack. He had attempted to persuade Göring to allow him to make use of his experience as a dive-bomber pilot by forming a highly mobile Ju 88 unit ready for quick deployment to any front. In early September 1942 this idea came to fruition with the formation of I./KG 60.

4./KG 66, however, would use the combined experience of the *E.Kdo der Lw. 188*/KG 6 and 2.(*Ausb. u. Erp.*)/KG 60 personnel to take the Ju 188E-1 into operations 'in force'. In reality, it would join a curtailed Luftwaffe bomber arm which, during the second half of 1943, was capable only of mounting *Störangriffe* (nuisance attacks) against Britain.

Indeed, senior British commanders did not believe they had much to fear from a conventional Luftwaffe bomber campaign against the British Isles, although the threat was not totally ruled out. As former Fighter Command staff officer and military historian Basil Collier commented post-war;

'There was little disposition to over-estimate the threat from orthodox bombers, for the German bomber force had been unimpressive in recent months, and the training of crews for accurate bombing of well-defended targets was justly thought to have been so long neglected that a spectacular recovery was improbable.'

However, reports began to filter through that Dietrich Peltz was gathering a new force whose goal was to target London, which would be seen as the centre of command for any Allied invasion of occupied France, or places where troops, ships and aircraft could be expected to assemble during the spring, though even these reports caused little alarm among the staffs of RAF Fighter Command and the Air Defence of Great Britain.

Promoted to oberstleutnant on 1 December 1942, Peltz was ordered away from operations with I./KG 60 and appointed *General der Kampfflieger*. In March 1943, he was simultaneously given the title *Angriffsführer England* (Attack Leader England), with specific responsibility for assembling a bomber force and effecting a bombing campaign against the British Isles. In August 1943, as Peltz was preparing for this, he was appointed commander of IX. *Fliegerkorps* and promoted to oberst. Peltz had no easy task ahead of him. As at 30 September, the bomber strength of *Luftflotte* 3, the German air fleet in France, comprising Do 217s, Me 410s, Ju 88s, Ju 188s, Fw 200s and He 177s, was just 122 aircraft, of which 104 were serviceable.

Although it has been the subject of debate among Luftwaffe historians, one of the first – possibly the first – deployment of Ju 188s over England came on the night of 17–18 August 1943, when a force of 55 Do 217s from I./KG 2 was assigned to strike at a factory in Lincoln, while 13 Me 410s from V./KG 2 undertook a *Fernnachtjagd* in the Cambridge area. At least 25 aircraft are believed to have operated over the more northern reaches of eastern England, with target and turning point marking being provided by Do 217s of 1./KG 66. According to (the then) Leutnant Hans Altrogge of I./KG 66, a small number of Ju 188s undertook a *Horcheinsatz* (listening operation) to monitor British radio and radar activity during the raid.

In late April–early May 1943, 15./KG 6, which was a He 111/Do 217-equipped pathfinder unit formed from selected and experienced crews from the likes of KG 100 and led by Hauptmann Rudolf Mohrmann, began to re-equip to form the nucleus of the new I./KG 66 at Chartres, in France, under Major Hermann Schmidt, a staff officer assigned from Peltz's *Angriffsführer England*. Mohrmann's *Staffel* would provide cadres for 1., 2. and 3./KG 66, with the first two of these *Staffeln* intended as illuminators and the third as a specialist electronic warfare unit. At Chartres, the *Gruppe* began to replace its Do 217s with Ju 88S-1s, as well as a small number of Ju 188s. I./KG 66 moved to Montdidier, in France, in June, from where it would operate all three types for a period, and where it would remain until March 1944.

A Ju 188E-1 probably from I./KG 66 undergoes maintenance at Montdidier in the autumn of 1943, when the *Gruppe* mounted its first sorties with the new bomber against Britain. In a move to increase speed for their 'pathfinding' and 'illuminator' roles, some of the unit's Ju 188s were flown devoid of the upper gun dome. Note also the *'Kuto-Nase'* steel cutter frame mounted around the forward part of the nose, black-painted undersides for nocturnal operations and the segmented spinner (*EN Archive*)

For the mission to Lincoln, the Ju 188s may have been under the command of Oberleutnant Helmut Schmid. Some sources state that they marked out the Lincoln works of the diesel engine and locomotive manufacturer Ruston and Hornsby, or at least acted as *Zielfinder* (target-markers) in some way, dropping marker or illumination flares at the turning points over the North Sea and the Lincolnshire coast at Gibraltar Point, augmenting similar operations performed by KG 2's own bombers.

In his *Leistungsbuch* (combat diary), Leutnant Altrogge, who took off at 2317 hrs, notes that the target was a 'Dieselmotorenwerk in Lincoln'. The Ju 188s flew a route from Soesterberg, in the Netherlands, to The Wash, in East Anglia, and then on to Lincoln, followed by a return course to Deelen, again in the Netherlands, maintaining altitudes of 800–5000 m over the target area. Enemy nightfighters were encountered in the climbing area over The Wash, as well as light, medium and heavy anti-aircraft fire. Altrogge's crew returned at 0239 hrs, exactly 202 minutes after they had left Soesterberg. The raid was not a success – no targets in Lincoln were hit, and KG 2 lost 11 Do 217s before, during or after it. However, as far as the Ju 188s were concerned, whether they were operating as the *E.Kdo der Lw. 188* or 1./KG 66, it seems that none were destroyed.

Altrogge would fly the Ju 188 just once more in 1943 (his other sorties were in a Ju 88S) when, on the morning of 2 July, he carried out a trouble-free *Horcheinsatz* from Schiphol, in the Netherlands, to Montdidier, probably to monitor Allied shipping in the English Channel.

In August, KG 6 had established its own *Erprobungsstaffel* with which to assess the Ju 188 tactically and to familiarise a select number of its airmen on the type. At the beginning of September, I./KG 6, based at Chièvres under the command of the operationally experienced Major Helmut Fuhrhop and having not long relocated to Belgium from the Mediterranean, started to re-equip with the Ju 188E-1 – the first full *Gruppe* to do so. Fuhrhop was a *Legion Condor* veteran who had seen service in the Balkans and Russia with KG 51. Transferring to KG 6 in January 1943, he took part in attacks on convoys off North Africa and was credited with the sinking of two 8000-ton freighters. These successes earned Fuhrhop the Knight's Cross on 22 November 1943.

I./KG 6 had been allocated 32 Ju 188E-1s but it only received 27 during the course of September, none of which were operationally ready. The unit also retained six Ju 88A-4s and two A-14s. By early October, however, 36 Ju 188s had been delivered, of which 19 were declared ready for operations. Two would be lost in crashes in the first days of the month during the working-up process.

Meanwhile, II./KG 2 was also taking on the Ju 188 at its base at Münster-Handorf, overseen by its *Kommandeur*, Major Heinz Engel (previously *Kapitän* of 5./KG 2), and the unit would also soon be operational.

It would not be long before I./KG 6 commenced operations against Britain with its new aircraft. On the night of 2–3 October, Ju 188s from 1. *Staffel* carried out a mining operation over the Humber. Although all of the 1./KG 6 aircraft returned unscathed, Ju 188 Z6+GK, flown by Leutnant Günther Beubler of 2./KG 66 in the role of *Zielfinder* for this mission, crashed into a mud bank close to the lighthouse at Spurn Head while attempting to evade an enemy nightfighter.

Air- and groundcrew gather around the access hatch of a Ju 188E, possibly of KG 6, at Chièvres. Note the ETC 500/IXd bomb rack under the starboard inner wing and the A-*Stand* cartridge ejection port for the MG 151 nose-mounted cannon in the lower starboard nose aft of the *Lotfe* 7D bombsight viewing port (*Carrick*)

During the night of 7–8 October, IX. *Fliegerkorps* sent 36 of its bombers to attack London, while 28 others headed to Norwich, in Norfolk. At least some aircraft from I./KG 6 carried SC 1000 bombs, as well as SC 50s. Although nightfighters were encountered, all the *Geschwader*'s aircraft returned, without loss, to Chièvres. A Ju 188 from 2./KG 66 did fail to return, however.

I./KG 6 completed its re-equipment with Ju 188s on 10 October, but five days later it would suffer a heavy blow. During the foggy afternoon of the 15th, seven of the *Gruppe*'s more experienced crews drawn from 1. and 3. *Staffeln* were selected and briefed to fly a mission to London that night. Given the weather conditions, this caused some surprise and trepidation. As a consequence of the fog over Belgium, the Netherlands and France, it was decided to use Münster-Handorf as the starting point for the mission. The problem was that there were no bombs available there, and so the intermediate landing at Münster-Handorf from Chièvres would have to be made with the ordnance loaded – hence the requirement for the best crews. Each Ju 188 would be laden with two SC 1000 HE bombs and ten SC 50s.

The outward route was planned as a low-level flight from Münster-Handorf to the Hook of Holland, then a climbing flight over the North Sea to around 11,000 m in order to cross the English coast near Harwich, in Essex. From the crossing point, the Ju 188s would turn directly for London, bomb the capital from around 7000 m, then turn and head for Margate, in Kent. Crossing the coast outbound, crews would descend from 5000 m down to sea level and maintain that altitude all the way back to Münster-Handorf.

Ultimately, just four of the *Gruppe*'s new Ju 188s operated individually over London between 2008 and 2311 hrs from altitudes of between 5000–7000 m, and the effects could not be observed. Two of the crews also attacked alternative targets at Southend, in Essex, and Harwich. However, trouble awaited them in the form of Mosquito nightfighters of No 85 Sqn based at West Malling, in Kent. This unit had at least two of its aircraft up on patrol over the coasts of Kent and East Anglia between 2215 hrs on the 15th and 0050 hrs on the 16th.

Sqn Ldr W H (Bill) Maguire and his navigator/radar operator, Flg Off W D (Bill) Jones, had left West Malling at 2215 hrs and were soon directed by their control at Sandwich, in Kent, to a 'Bandit' at a range of 20 miles in the Ipswich, Suffolk, area. Maguire closed to within 2000 ft at a height of 18,000 ft, and as he did so, the enemy aircraft made a hard, diving turn to port. As the Mosquito turned inside of its quarry, Maguire spotted 'the silhouette of pointed wings and black crosses' and identified it provisionally as a Ju 188. His identification was correct, for this was E-1 Wk-Nr 260197 3E+FL flown by Hauptmann Helmut Waldecker, the *Staffelkapitän* of 3./KG 6.

Maguire opened fire on the Ju 188 at 250 yards and closed to 100 yards, observing strikes to the port engine, which burst into flames. Waldecker continued to turn and then attempted to climb to starboard, but lost height. The Mosquito went in pursuit, and Maguire fired another burst from 50 yards, after which the enemy aircraft 'fell out of the sky burning well'. By the light of the flames, Maguire had a good view of the aircraft's rounded cockpit, and revised his identification to that of an Me 410, 'but possibly a Ju 188'. The bomb-laden 3E+FL crashed into marshland and exploded at Kirton Creek, a mile south of the village of Hemley to the east of Ipswich.

Waldecker, saved by his seat armour, and his observer, Obergefreiter Waldemar Haupt, who had been slightly cut by shell splinters, were able to bail out after some frantic moments trying to unjam the escape hatch as the Junkers plummeted towards the earth. They were later captured, but radio operator Unteroffizier Karl-Heinz Müller, who had suffered a head wound and whose left arm had been shot off, and gunner, Oberfeldwebel Julius Hohmann, who had received severe wounds to his leg and who had lost consciousness in the air, were both killed. Waldecker and Haupt had pushed Hohmann through the hatch, pulling his parachute D-ring as he went out, but it was in vain.

Moments later, Maguire and Jones were given another 'Bandit' heading west at a range of eight miles. Contact was obtained and Maguire climbed from 18,000 ft to 23,000 ft, closing to within 1500 ft of the enemy aircraft, at which point it pulled up and peeled off to port. Again, Maguire thought he had encountered a second Me 410, but in fact this was Ju 188E-1 Wk-Nr 260173 3E+IH, flown by Leutnant Wolfgang Haeyn of 1./KG 6.

Maguire followed the contact visually, as it was highlighted against a light cloud background, and when he had closed to within 1000 ft he opened fire. The enemy aircraft returned fire, but the gunnery was 'very wild and inaccurate and badly directed'. The German machine turned sharply to port, but the Mosquito closed again to within 100 yards. Maguire fired again, and he observed strikes on the starboard engine and centre fuselage, which burst into flames. The enemy aircraft dived towards the sea 'burning well' and causing 'a very extensive glow through the cloud layer as it hit the deck and exploded' at 2310 hrs off Clacton-on-Sea, in Essex.

The cheerful crew of a Ju 188E fitted with a '*Kuto-Nase*' steel cutter frame refer to a route map in what is most probably a posed photograph. All the men wear two-piece 'Kanal' (Channel) flight suits, so-named colloquially by crews engaged in operations over the English Channel and distinctive for the large 'bellows' pockets on the trousers. They also wear pneumatic inflatable life jackets, and the type of compressed air cylinder used for these can be clearly seen on the jacket of the man at far right. The crewman second from right wears a standard fleece-lined leather flying helmet (*Carrick*)

Haeyn, his observer Unteroffizier Josef Schams and radio operator Unteroffizier Franz Mary were posted as missing, while gunner Unteroffizier Herbert Fickert was registered as killed.

Five minutes later, Flg Off H B Thomas and his navigator/radar operator WO C B Hamilton encountered Ju 188 Wk-Nr 260171 3E+HH flown by Leutnant Karl Geyr of 1./KG 6 over the north Kent coast, the aircraft almost certainly homeward-bound heading for Margate and the sea beyond. At 12,000 ft, Thomas obtained contact on Geyr on an almost 'head-on' course. He duly made a 'climbing turn to reciprocal and climbed full throttle from 12,000 to 21,000 ft, where a visual was obtained well above'.

It was at this point that Thomas realised his Mosquito was silhouetted against the ten-tenths cloud below, so he turned away 'down moon'. Minutes later he reversed his course and climbed back up, regaining contact. Aware of the Mosquito's presence, Geyr took evasive action by steeply diving away, with the nightfighter about a mile behind him as the two aircraft followed the line of the coast. Geyr then applied full power and climbed, before diving away again and making a few turns as he lost altitude. Thomas and Hamilton were only able to gain a few 'fleeting visuals' of their target due to its manoeuvring. However, at between 15,000 and 11,000 ft, Thomas closed the distance to 300 yards and got off four bursts of 20 mm cannon fire, before closing in to just 80 yards. As the No 85 Sqn combat report later stated;

'Strikes were seen on the port engine from the first burst, the starboard engine started to smoke with the second one, the third missed, and large pieces fell off the port wing and engine from the fourth burst.'

The Ju 188 fell steeply away to starboard with both of its engines trailing flames and crashed at St Nicholas at Wade, three miles southwest of Birchington-on-Sea, in Kent. Geyr survived to be taken prisoner, but his observer, Feldwebel Walter Flessner, was killed and his radio operator, Obergefreiter Dietram Kretschmar, and gunner, Obergefreiter Otto Schmidt, were posted missing.

Flt Lt Cecil 'Jimmy' Rawnsley, who flew with high-scoring nightfighter ace Wg Cdr John 'Cat's Eyes' Cunningham in No 85 Sqn, commented in his memoirs on the encounters his squadron had with Ju 188s and Me 410s at this time;

'Our targets were nearly all fast, highly elusive customers, and the pressure was beginning to tell on our hard-driven engines. They had been persistently flogged over a period of months, and they were beginning to crack up in the middle of chases.'

Throughout November and December operations against Britain by Ju 188 units would be sporadic when compared to those mounted by units

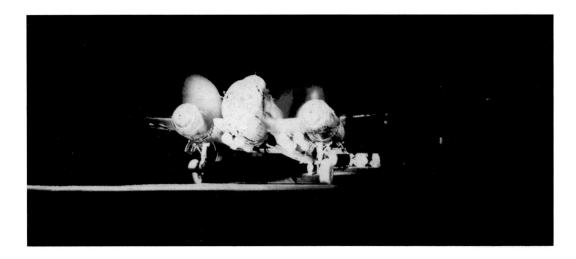

equipped with the Ju 88 and Do 217. This was attributable in part to low serviceability and the ongoing processes of conversion, familiarisation and training on what was still regarded as a new type by II./KG 2 at Münster-Handorf.

Nevertheless, the *Erprobungsstaffel*, now under the command of Knight's Cross-holder Oberleutnant Hans Mader, and I./KG 6 did continue to despatch small numbers of Ju 188s on probing, nuisance raids, usually as part of larger incursions. During the evening of 31 October, for example, 12 Ju 188s from the *Gruppe* operated as *Beleuchter* ('illuminators', dropping flares) for aircraft of III./KG 6 carrying out a *Störangriff* on London. Despite searchlights, light and heavy anti-aircraft fire and the presence of nightfighters, the Ju 188s made it back.

During the late afternoon of the following day, 12 Ju 188s were assigned to undertake dusk nuisance raids along the south coast of England, with the focus on Southampton, in Hampshire, and Hastings and Newhaven, in East Sussex. The weather was not good and bombing was to be carried out through cloud using *Knickebein* radar assistance. Eventually, as the Ju 188s were over the English Channel, they were ordered to return. Seven turned back, but five aircraft continued to England. The Southampton force was led by the Ju 188s of Leutnante Hans-Friedrich Lenkeit and Christoph Hanzig, both from 2./KG 6. Their aircraft were each loaded with two SC 1000, two SC 500 and ten SC 50 bombs. Lenkeit was forced to abort the mission because of the deteriorating weather and return to Chièvres, but the others pressed on and bombed between 1940–1822 hrs, despite the weather, anti-aircraft fire and nightfighter defence.

F.-1 Wk-Nr 260198 3E+CL from 3. *Staffel*, flown by Berliner Leutnant Kurt Reckin, who had served with the unit since joining it at Foggia in early July, crashed at Church Farm near Maiden Bradley, in Wiltshire, probably as a result of navigational difficulties in the adverse conditions. The aircraft had descended, circling through the low cloud and rain. It released its load of 12 bombs, but then flew over the slope of a steep hill, dived vertically into the ground and was destroyed. The crew of Reckin, Unteroffiziere Walter Overhoff (observer), Karl-Heinz Siegler (radio operator) and Karl Weisskamp (gunner) were killed.   (*text continues on page 45*)

With its BMW 801 engines running, a Ju 188E of II./KG 2 taxies out close to airfield buildings for another night mission, probably from Münster-Handorf. The aircraft is armed with an MG 151 in the nose and has bombs suspended from its inner wing undersurfaces (*EN Archive*)

1
Ju 188 V1 (Ju 88 V44) Wk-Nr 1687 NF+KQ, possibly at *Erprobungsstelle* Rechlin, Germany, 1942

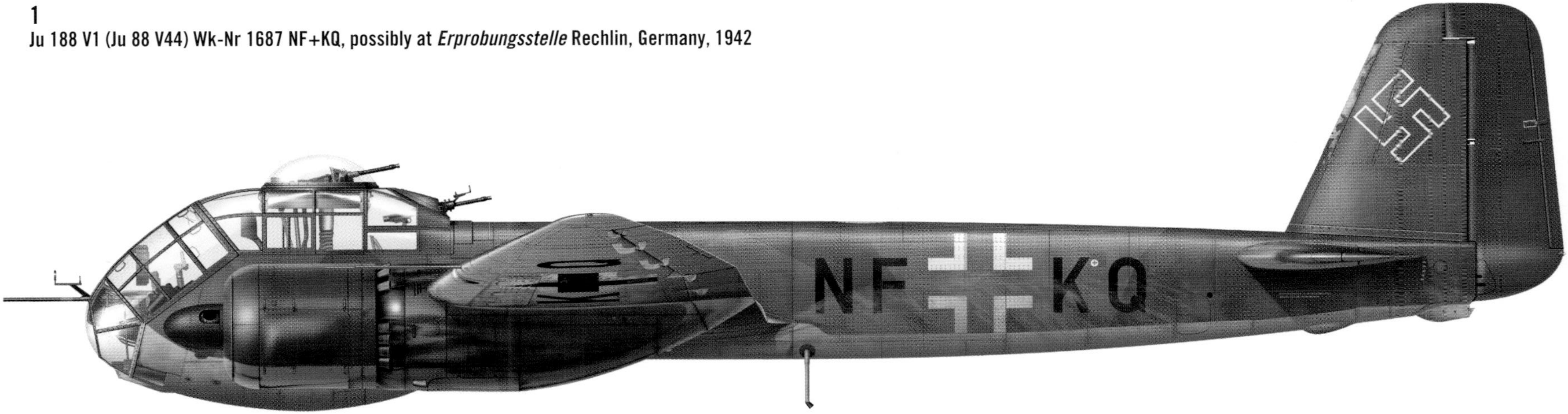

2
Ju 188E-0 Wk-Nr 10001 CG+CE, Junkers AG, Bernburg, Germany, spring 1943

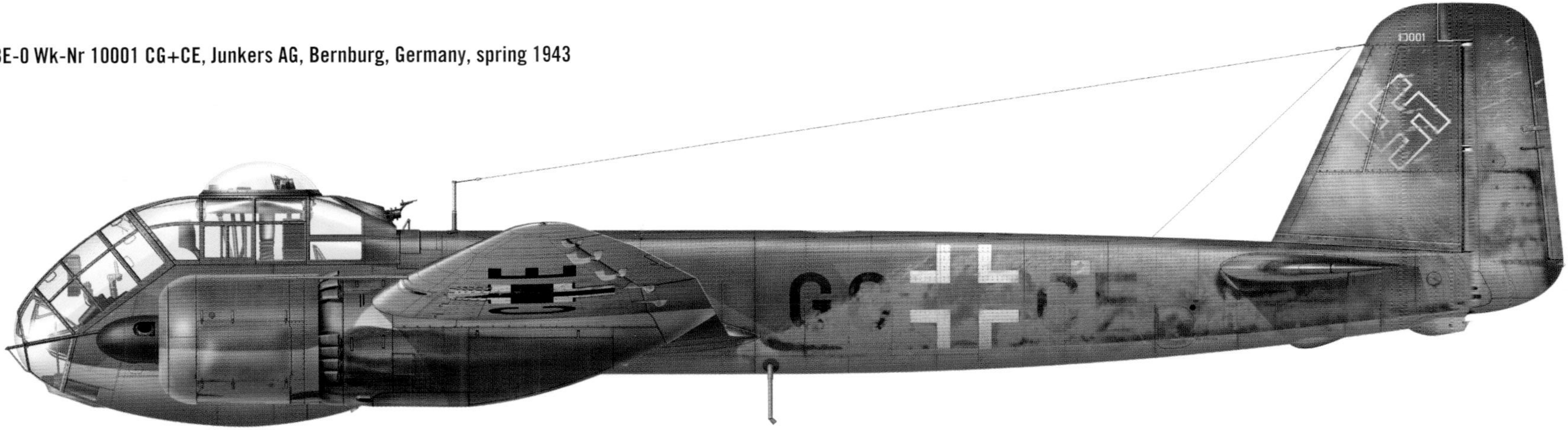

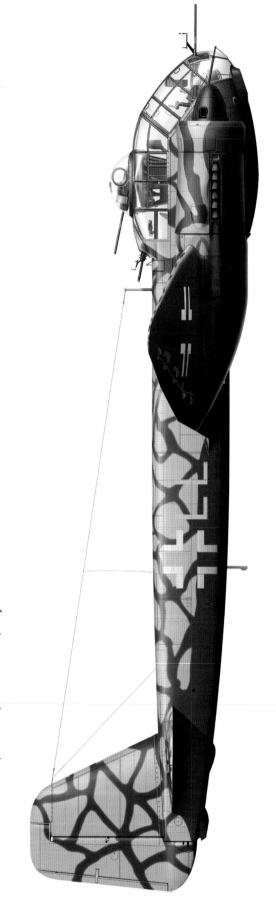

3
Ju 188A-2 U5+LL of 3./KG 2, Eindhoven, the Netherlands, early 1944

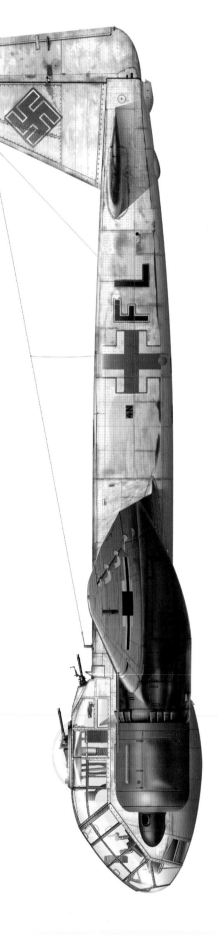

4
Ju 188F-1 4N+FL of 3.(F)/22, northern Russia, early 1944

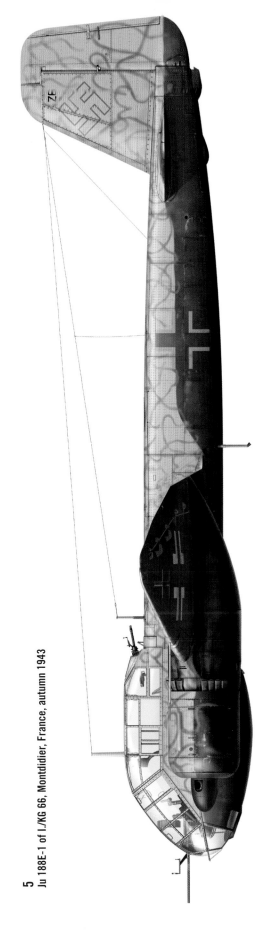

5
Ju 188E-1 of I./KG 66, Montdidier, France, autumn 1943

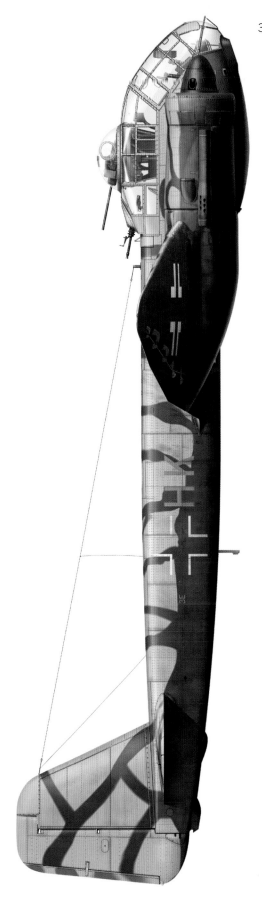

6
Ju 188A-2 3E+HK of 2./KG 6, Brussels-Melsbroek, Belgium, 1944

36

7
Ju 188A ??+RM, unit unknown, France, 1944

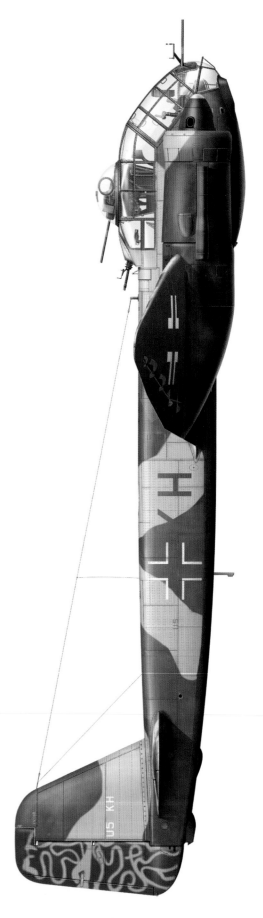

8
Ju 188A-2 U5+KH of 1./KG 2, Lyon-Bron, France, 1944

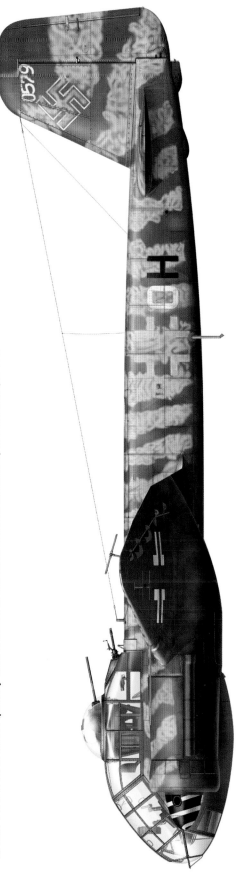

9
Ju 188D-1 or D-2 Wk-Nr ??0579 (possibly 150579) 8H+OH of 1./AufKl.Gr. 33, northern Germany or Denmark, April 1945

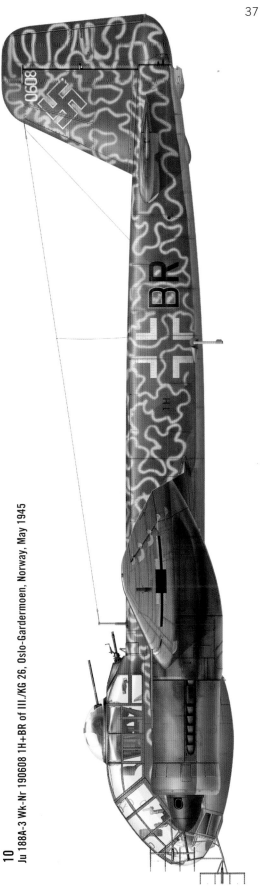

10
Ju 188A-3 Wk-Nr 190608 1H+BR of III./KG 26, Oslo-Gardermoen, Norway, May 1945

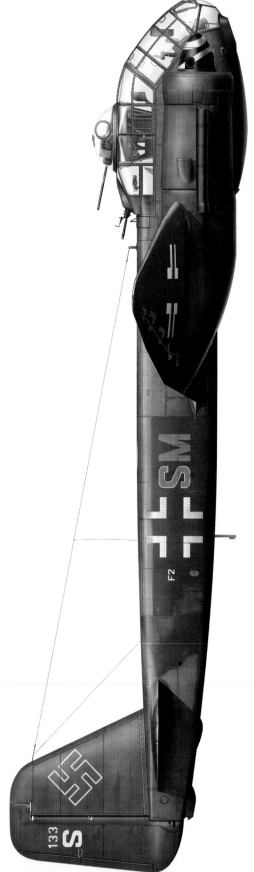

11
Ju 188D Wk-Nr (???)133 F2+SM possibly of 4./Erg.FAGr. 4, Braunschweig area, Germany, April–May 1945

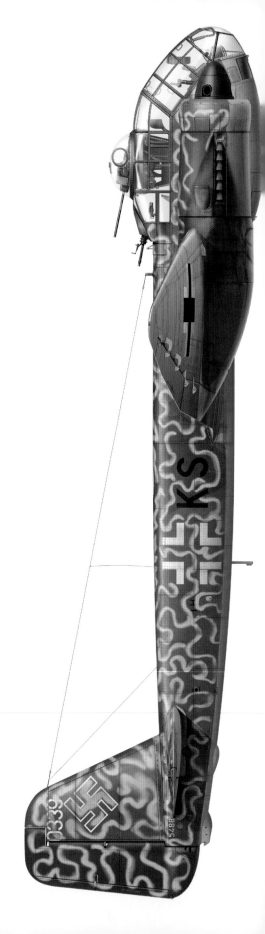

12
Ju 188A Wk-Nr 190339 1H+KS III./KG 26, Copenhagen-Kastrup, Denmark, 1945

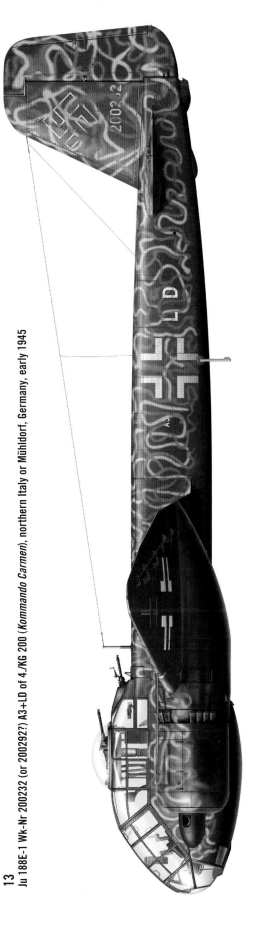

13
Ju 188E-1 Wk-Nr 200232 (or 200292?) A3+LD of 4./KG 200 (*Kommando Carmen*), northern Italy or Mühldorf, Germany, early 1945

14
Ju 188D-1(?) Wk-Nr 230424 9A+LM, unit unknown, US zone of operations, May 1945

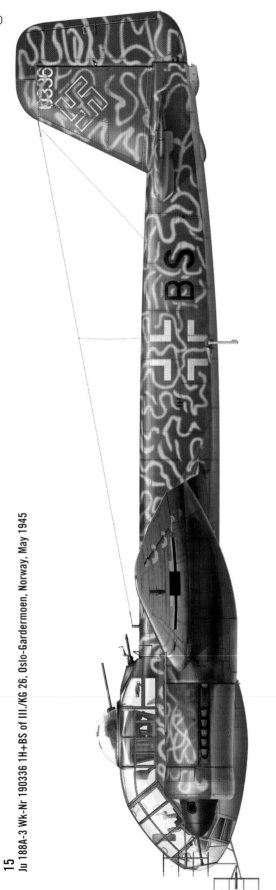

15
Ju 188A-3 Wk-Nr 190336 1H+BS of III./KG 26, Oslo-Gardermoen, Norway, May 1945

16
Ju 188D-2 7A+MM of 4.(F)/121, Hradec-Králové, Czechoslovakia, April 1945

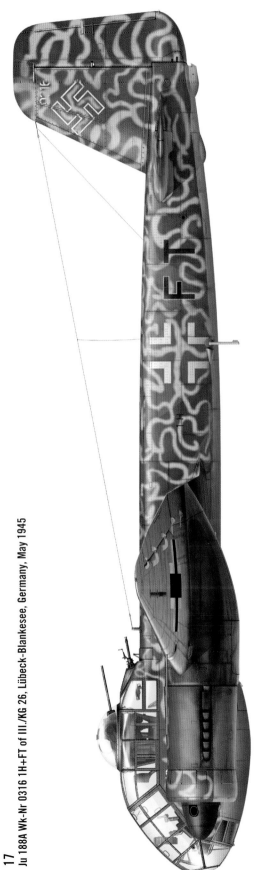

17
Ju 188A Wk-Nr 0316 1H+FT of III./KG 26, Lübeck-Blankesee, Germany, May 1945

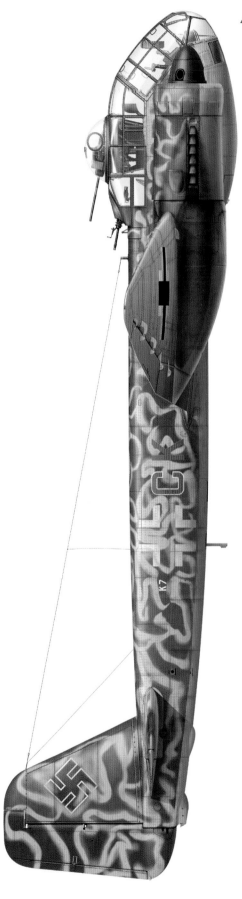

18
Ju 188D-2 Wk-Nr 230422 K7+CK of *Aufklärungsstaffel* 2.(F)/*Nacht*, Marienlyst-Østersøbad, Denmark, May 1945

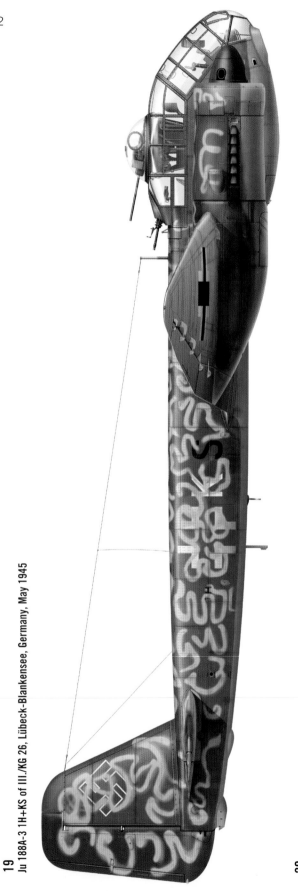

19
Ju 188A-3 1H+KS of III./KG 26, Lübeck-Blankensee, Germany, May 1945

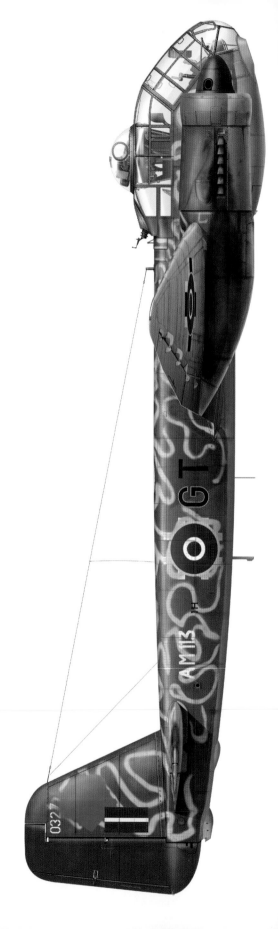

20
Ju 188A-3 Wk-Nr 190327 1H+GT formerly of III./KG 26, RAE Farnborough, England, August 1945

21
Ju 388 V8/L-0 Wk-Nr 300002 PG+YB, Junkers AG Merseburg and *Erprobungsstelle* Rechlin, Germany, early 1944

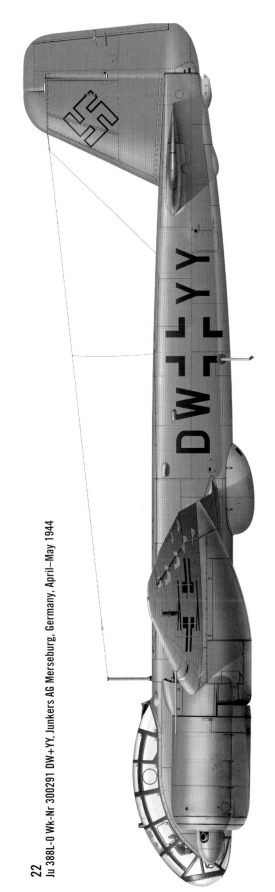

22
Ju 388L-0 Wk-Nr 300291 DW+YY, Junkers AG Merseburg, Germany, April–May 1944

44

23
Ju 388K-0 Wk-Nr 230151 KS+TA, Junkers AG Merseburg, Germany, May–June 1944

24
Ju 388L-1 Wk-Nr 560049, Junkers AG Merseburg, May 1945

Elsewhere, Ju 188E-1 Wk-Nr 1000 3E+AF, of the *Erprobungsstaffell/ KG 6*, flown by Oberleutnant Helmut Schmid – one of the first Luftwaffe pilots to train up on the aircraft – was endeavouring to make its way out of England, but again the weather may have played its part in sending the bomber off course. At 1755 hrs, Flt Lt S F Hodsman and WO A F Monger of No 29 Sqn were scrambled in their Mosquito from Ford, in West Sussex, to intercept the *Störangriff*, which at that time was reported as approaching the coast from 30 miles out to sea. Taking instructions from a GCI controller, Hodsman and Monger climbed to 15,000 ft and were then directed north away from the coast. They were further instructed to descend to 10,000 ft, as a target had been picked up four miles ahead, with range rapidly decreasing. Almost at the same moment, the RAF crew acquired a contact and visual some 3000 ft above them and about a mile away.

Hodsman managed to climb to within 1000 ft below and behind before Schmid's crew became aware of the Mosquito's presence. In the Ju 188, it was probably the gunner, Unteroffizier Josef Koidl, who opened fire with the C-*Stand* MG 81Z. According to the subsequent RAF combat report;

'The fire from the E/A [enemy aircraft] came close over the top of Mosquito and then [the Ju 188] immediately dived steeply, weaving violently, with Mosquito on his tail closing in gradually. The Tit was pulled but did not operate and Mosquito fired 4 or 5 short bursts closing from about 3000 ft, till the final burst at about 1000 ft. Height had been lost down to Angels 2. Strikes were seen on the wing outboard of the port engine and a large red flash between fuselage and starboard engine. There were 4 or 5 bursts of return fire probably from the dorsal position, accurate for line, but above Mosquito. After the final burst, E/A had reached cloud at 2000 ft and disappeared suddenly. No further contact obtained.'

In the rapidly diminishing daylight, local farmworkers watched as the damaged Ju 188 emerged from cloud and flew into the side of Walbury Hill at Combe, in Berkshire. Schmid, his observer, Oberfeldwebel Bruno Krupp, radio operator Stabsfeldwebel Erich Zuch and gunner Unteroffizier Josef Koidl were killed.

The defenders did not always have it their way, however. A good Ju 188 gunner could make his mark even on a Mosquito, as happened over the

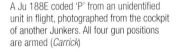
A Ju 188E coded 'P' from an unidentified unit in flight, photographed from the cockpit of another Junkers. All four gun positions are armed (*Carrick*)

English Channel, some 30 miles south of Dungeness, in Kent, on the night of 6–7 November. Sqn Ldr John Selway and his navigator/radar operator Plt Off Norman Bamford of No 85 Sqn had taken off from West Malling on a patrol in a Mosquito at 2235 hrs. They had been vectored towards an 'Fw 190', which they had shot down in flames south of Hastings at 2355 hrs. They were then given a second vector on another 'Bandit' heading south about 20 miles away. The Mosquito closed to 6000 ft, but the enemy aircraft was so far below that Selway could not have descended sufficiently without overshooting, so he turned to starboard, then back to port.

Contact was regained on what was believed to have been a Ju 188 'travelling very fast and weaving at about 20,000 ft'. Selway closed to some 1000 ft, but with range decreasing very rapidly, so Bamford told his pilot to throttle back. At that moment a burst of fire from the Ju 188 hit Selway, inflicting a serious wound to his stomach, and he was unable to return fire. The pilot lost control and the Mosquito went into a dive, the engagement abandoned. Despite his wound, Selway managed to level the nightfighter off and land it back at West Malling, with his airspeed indicator and altimeter having been shot up as a result of a bullet entering the cockpit between the windscreen and the armour plate below it, which then smashed into the instrument panel. After landing, Selway walked into the crewroom unaided, and as Jimmy Rawnsley later wrote;

'For a while he just stood there discussing the affair with the others in his usual light-hearted fashion. He started to drink some tea, but fortunately "Rigor" Mortimer snatched the cup away from him, thereby possibly saving his life. When he started to undress, the onlookers were shocked to see that his clothes were liberally soaked in blood.'

Selway was immediately taken to hospital, where, in an emergency operation, the tip of a bullet from the Ju 188 was removed from his liver. He survived, but it was the end of his second tour.

The Ju 188s of I./KG 66 were also operating as target-finders. On the night of 15 November four of them flew to Plymouth with 36 Do 217s from KG 2. This force dropped just over 55 tons of high explosive and incendiary bombs on the naval port, but one of the Ju 188s failed to return.

Ju 188E-1s from I./KG 6 mounted further nuisance raids to London on 2 December. During the morning, around 20 aircrews were hurriedly called to a briefing by the *Gruppenkommandeur*, Major Fuhrhop. The plan was to take advantage of the heavy cloud over England and attack the East End of London in a rare daylight operation. The choice of specific targets would be left to the crews, but the priority was industry.

In one sortie, two Ju 188s headed out, one flown by Unteroffizier Alfred Popp and the other by Unteroffizier Heinrich Gerst, both of 1. *Staffel*. Although Gerst soon lost visual contact with

A Ju 188E of I./KG 66 in the *Gruppe*'s customary grey/black camouflage. Such aircraft dropped marker flares during raids on Britain in the autumn of 1943 and in the later *Steinbock* attacks (*EN Archive*)

Popp's bomber, he pressed on towards London. No German aircraft were encountered during the rest of the mission, although intense anti-aircraft fire targeted the lone bomber between the English coast and the capital. Fighters also pursued Gerst's Ju 188 through the clouds, but the crew evaded them, carried out their mission and turned for home, returning shortly before midday. Unteroffizier Popp and his crew would not be so fortunate.

At 1026 hrs, two Typhoons from No 181 Sqn flown by Flt Sgts Grey and Kenneth Hanna were scrambled from Merston, in West Sussex, on a defensive patrol. Hanna, a Canadian, flying as No 2 became separated from Grey in cloud. As he later reported;

'About 7 or 8 minutes after taking off, I saw a Do 217, camouflaged black, 2000/1500 yards dead ahead crossing at 60 degrees, and as I closed in the e/a started to take evasive action. I opened fire at 500/700 yards with a 2-second burst from 90 to 60 degrees, using 80 rounds of 20 mm ammunition. The e/a turned to port, and thick black smoke was seen pouring from the starboard engine as it disappeared into cloud and was not seen again. No return fire was experienced from e/a.'

Hanna claimed a 'damaged', but his victim was most probably Ju 188E-1 Wk-Nr 260168 3E+EH flown by Unteroffizier Popp, which is believed to have crashed into the Channel with the loss of Popp and his crew of Obergefreiter Ewald Scherff (observer), Obergefreiter Manfred Forst (radio operator) and Obergefreiter Helmut Kunze (gunner).

Another Ju 188E-1 from 2./KG 6 was hit by anti-aircraft fire and crashed into the sea off South Foreland, in Kent, at exactly the same time Flt Sgt Hanna took off in his Typhoon from Merston. Wk-Nr 260199 3E+DK had been the third aircraft to leave Chièvres just after 0900 hrs. The crew, comprising pilot Fahnenjunker-Feldwebel Johann Schwarz, observer Gefreiter Erich Schulze, radio operator Unteroffizier Alois Wenzel and gunner Gefreiter Herbert Simon, were on their first mission.

They flew west-southwest from Chièvres at an altitude of just 400 ft and reached the French coast near Le Touquet. After following the coast as far as Dieppe, they headed for London and, flying on a zigzag course, climbed steadily to cross the English coast at a height of about 13,000 ft. Whilst flying at this altitude in ten-tenths cloud, they were subjected to anti-aircraft fire for some ten minutes, during which time Schwarz took violent evasive action. Perhaps inevitably, an explosion followed, and the aircraft began to fall through the air with pieces of it breaking away. The survivors came down in the sea, and three of them – Schwarz, Schulze and Simon – were recovered, but Unteroffizier Wenzel was posted missing. The survivors were surprised to find themselves in the Dover area, having strayed considerably off course.

There was no doubt that such sporadic operations by the Ju 188 units were proving a nuisance to British air and ground defences and causing alarm to the civilian population in southern England, but they were also proving hazardous to the Junkers' crews, and losses were high in proportion to the effort committed. Oberst Peltz was doing the best he could with the meagre resources available to him. However, far from any relaxation of this strategy on the part of the Luftwaffe, in the coming weeks the intensity of bombing operations was to increase further so that more decisive results could be achieved. It remained to be seen whether such an initiative would yield success.

CHAPTER FOUR

FROM THE ARCTIC TO AFRICA

From early 1944, production commenced at Leipzig-Mockau and Bernburg on the overdue Ju 188A series fitted with the long-awaited Jumo 213A-1 12-cylinder, liquid-cooled, inverted, inline engine. The A variant had been intended as a bomber as far back as June 1943, when, for armament, the A-1 was planned as having an MG 151 in the A-*Stand*, an MG 131 in the B2-*Stand* and an MG 81Z in the C-*Stand*. As an alternative, the A-2 was to carry an MG 151 in the B2-*Stand* and an MG 131 in the C-*Stand*.

Although appearing sequentially after the E, the A-model incorporated several of the later refinements and improvements that featured in the E-1. Although smaller than the Jumo 211, the Jumo 213 had an edge in terms of performance thanks to its pressurised cooling system – with high boost settings, it was designed to produce 1750 hp at 3250 rpm. The engine had a strengthened crankshaft and block, and its two-speed, two-stage supercharger enhanced performance at altitude. This made the Jumo 213 the ideal powerplant for an aircraft tasked with undertaking high-altitude bombing and reconnaissance missions. In late 1943, its performance was improved still further with MW (methanol water) 50 injection, which gave 2200 hp at take-off. This formed the basis for the Ju 188A-2, which became the main production variant.

Oberleutnant Peter Stahl, who flew the Jumo-powered Ju 188 with KG 200, wrote of it;

Although posed, this is an excellent photograph of what could be a Ju 188F-1, coded 5M+D?, of 4.(F)/11 during that unit's conversion to the type from the Ju 88D at Gutenfeld in the early autumn of 1943. The aircraft is fully armed, with an MG 151 in the A-*Stand*, an MG 131 in the B2-*Stand* and an MG 81Z in the B1-*Stand*. The cartridge belt for the MG 151 on its Lafette L151/3 mount is visible. Note the groundcrewman sat atop the fuselage holding the hose leading from the tanker, indicating that this is an aircraft fitted with *Rüstsatz* B1 and/or B2 long-range internal tanks (*Carrick*)

'The two Jumo 213A-1 engines with their total of 3500 hp take-off power almost made this unladen bird into a sports aircraft, giving all of us an exhilarating feeling.'

The albeit limited operational experience gained with the E-1 bomber by the end of 1943 showed that the Ju 188 was best suited to level day and, more frequently, night bombing, and so the fitment of underwing dive brakes was discontinued. Otherwise, externally, the Ju 188A was similar in appearance to the E. Alongside the A came the D, intended as a reconnaissance aircraft. The D emulated the A, with the D-1 and D-2 versions fitted with similar armament sets as the A-1 and A-2.

Thus by early 1944, the Ju 188 was being produced in two main engine variants which, in turn, had two sub-variants fundamentally based on mission type and armament.

Meanwhile, along with the E-1 bomber, construction and equipment details for the Ju 188F-1 long-range reconnaissance aircraft were contained in the joint *Baubeschreibung* of January 1943. During the mid-war years, it became clear that, in the face of increasingly alert and strengthened enemy defences, speed and altitude were essential for the safe collection of aerial photographs. The Ju 188 fitted the bill. Essentially, the four-seat F-1 was similar to the bomber variant in respect to its build and basic equipment, and it was powered by BMW 801D radial engines.

Cameras were installed in the rear fuselage between Frames 15 and 20, just forward of the compartment where the radio and blind-landing system boxes were installed. For daylight missions, two Rb (*Reihenbilder* – row or series picture) 50/30 or 75/30 cameras were positioned with lenses facing downwards to glazed panes in the fuselage floor, to which were attached sliding covers. All cameras had a two- or three-letter designator, followed by a series of numbers separated by a diagonal slash. The first two numbers indicated the focal length of the lens, usually 20, 30, 50 or 75 cm, with the numbers following the slash identifying the exposure size made by the camera. Thus, the Rb 50/30 signified a 50 cm lens, producing a 30 cm exposure.

The narrow, neat frontal profile of the Ju 188F-1 is seen here as an aircraft of 3. (F)/33 makes a low approach across the beach near Kalamaki on its return from a convoy reconnaissance sortie (*Wadman*)

The Rb 50/30 mapping camera was fitted with an iris inter-lens shutter and, with a full magazine loaded with 64 m of film and associated attachments, weighed approximately 72 kg. In addition, and in contrast to contemporary aerial camera/film applications, the film in the Zeiss Rb series of cameras was held flat in the exposure position by means of dynamic air pressure supplied from a blower fan powered via the camera drive motor. The latter, with both fans and heating elements, was also fitted in the Ju 188's camera bay. For night missions, NRb 40/25 or 50/25 cameras were used.

The cameras were operated via a switchboard on the starboard side cockpit wall control board where bombing controls were to be found in the E-1. There was also an image sequence regulator located between the pilot and the radio operator.

The Ju 188F-1, and the follow-on F-2 powered by BMW 801G engines, could be fitted with FuG 200 ASV radar and FuG 217R tail warning equipment. The latter, weighing 27 kg, was not a standard fit, but some reconnaissance machines were so equipped.

By comparison, the Jumo-powered Ju 188D-1 had a camera installation based on the Ju 88D reconnaissance variant which saw the fitment of Rb 50/30 and Rb 20/30 cameras in various combinations mounted in the fuselage immediately aft of the bomb-bay. The Ju 188D-1 was also faster than the Ju 88D and had improved defensive armament.

Perhaps shaken, but not stirred. The crew of a Ju 188F-1 from 3.(F)/33 smile from their cockpit as they celebrate completion of their *Staffel*'s 1,000th operational mission, despite having crash-landed on the beach at Kalamaki. Note the sand covering the smashed nose canopy and the port spinner. A belt of ammunition hangs over the side of the cockpit (*Wadman*)

Ju 188 reconnaissance models (and some E-1 bombers) began to equip many Luftwaffe long-range *Aufklärungsstaffeln* from mid-1944. Usually, these units operated both F and D variants (except where indicated) and included *Stab*/FAGr 1 (Ju 188D-2 only), *Stab*/FAGr 2, *Stab*/FAGr 3 (D-2), 4.(F)/11, 4.(F)/14, 1. and 3.(F)/22, 1. and 3.(F)/33, 2.(F)/100, 1.(F)/120, 3. and 4.(F)/121, 3., 4., 5. and 6.(F)/122 (D-2s only except 6. *Staffel* which had F-1s), *Stab*, 1. and 6.(F)/ 123, and 1.(F)/124.

One of the first reconnaissance units to transition from the Ju 88A/D to the Ju 188F-1 was 3.(F)/33 under Oberleutnant Hans Bayer, which left Frosinone, in central Italy, to return to the Reich and convert at Königsberg-Devau in December 1943. By 2 February 1944 the Ob.d.L. *Führungsstab* was listing the *Staffel* as fully converted to the Ju 188 at Königsberg-Gutenfeld and under the tactical control of *Luftflotte Reich*, although reporting to the *General der Aufklärungsflieger*. It was further planned that in the event of any warning of an Allied invasion of Norway,

Probably a D-2, this Ju 188 of (F)/122 in 'meander' over-water camouflage returns to Ghedi following a reconnaissance mission over Italy, the Mediterranean or the Adriatic in 1944–45. The antennas for the FuG 101 radio altimeter can be seen under the port wing (*EN Archive*)

the *Staffel* was to move quickly to either Vaernes or Bardufoss. Similarly, should Turkey have entered the war on the side of the Allies, as part of Luftwaffe contingency plans, an *Oberbefehlshaber der Luftwaffe* (OKL – Luftwaffe High Command) document dated 15 March 1944 showed that the Ju 188s of 4.(F)/14 were to move to Sofia-Vrajdebna, in Bulgaria.

Ju 188F-1s first appeared in the Mediterranean in April 1944 when 3.(F)/33 commenced taking delivery of the type at Kalamaki, on the Greek island of Zakynthos, where their arrival coincided with the withdrawal of the Ju 88Ds of 1.(F)/122. 3.(F)/33 undertook operations from Kalamaki to Italy, Cyprus, Malta, Haifa, Alexandria and the Suez Canal. The *Staffel* celebrated a milestone when Oberleutnant Bayer and his crew flew the unit's 1000th mission,

The scene at Athens-Kalamaki in the spring of 1944. A Ju 188F-1 of 3.(F)/33 is parked in its brick revetment while Luftwaffe personnel chat in the sunshine nearby. The Ju 188F-1s of Hauptmann Hans Bayer's 3.(F)/33 operated from airfields in the Athens area between March and September 1944, undertaking reconnaissance of Allied convoys off North Africa and in the eastern Mediterranean (*Wadman*)

although they had to force-land their aircraft at Kalamaki as a result of damage sustained during the sortie. Bayer would lose his life on 12 April when Ju 188 8H+KL crashed into the harbour at Piraeus, in Greece. Along with Bayer, his crew of Leutnant Helms and Unteroffiziere Bergholz and Siebert were also lost.

1.(F)/33 was also active with Ju 188s by April 1944 from its base at Saint-Martin, 17 km northwest of Istres, in southern France, from where it carried out convoy reconnaissance off North Africa.

1.(F)/123 at Bergamo, in Italy, took on a pair of Ju 188D-2s to join its Ju 88T-1s in June for night-flying, although in reality these aircraft may have been operating with KG 200 (see later). Whatever the case, according to Allied signals intelligence Ju 188s were active on at least nine occasions, either on photographic missions or assisting weather reconnaissance unit *Wekusta* 26 on standard sea patrols. Throughout the summer of 1944, these aircraft covered the Ligurian Sea and the waters to the west and northwest of Corsica (both at day and night), as well as over the Adriatic as far south as Termoli, in Italy.

The number of Ju 188D-2s with 4.(F)/122 at Bergamo had increased to around 11 machines by June. The signals intelligence organisation of the Mediterranean Allied Air Forces (MAAF) noted that;

'This unit, though principally engaged in night missions, eventually resumed long distance daylight flights, which 1.(F)/123 had abandoned early in June. Evidently, the superiority of the Ju 188 over the Ju 88T made daylight reconnaissance of such danger spots as Corsica possible again.'

In July, the Ju 188s of 1.(F)/33 were particularly active over the Allied convoy route between Sicily and Benghazi, on the Libyan coast.

The one issue with the Ju 188 was the disparity in fuel grades required by the BMW 801 engines of the F and the Jumo 213 engines of the D. In the Mediterranean, the Junkers also tended to suffer from engine failures, and by the end of September 1944, most of the F variants had either been sent off to other units or required overhaul. By this stage, Ju 188s were parked up in revetments during the day, concealed by netting and tree foliage, and brought out for night missions just after dusk.

Single aircraft reconnaissance missions conducted over the vast tracts of the Eastern Front were of vital importance for German commanders, but highly dangerous for the crews involved. One unit to equip with the Ju 188 for reconnaissance was 2.(F)/100, which had previously flown Ju 88Ds over the southern USSR throughout the first half of 1943. One of its pilots was

Leutnant Helmut Reinert, who was awarded the *Frontflugspange in Gold* on 30 May 1944 after completing 110 reconnaissance missions. Here, he recalls how he narrowly avoided being shot down over Russia after his unit had converted to the Ju 188;

Mechanics service the starboard BMW 801 engine of a Ju 188F-1 of 3.(F)/33 in Greece in 1944. The aircraft appears to have provision for forward armament, and has a non-standard fairing over the cartridge ejection chute. The aircraft also has a *Kuto-Nase* device fitted around its nose (*Wadman*)

'By September 1943, our aircraft and crew losses on the Eastern Front had become excessive due to a significant improvement in Russian air defences. As the Ju 88 was primarily a medium-range "Stuka", and not at all suitable for long-distance reconnaissance assignments at high altitudes, our *Staffel*, 2.(F)/100, was taken out of action and sent to Königsberg-Gutenfeld to convert onto the new Ju 188. With the retraining of flight and maintenance crews and the refitting of the *Staffel* completed by the end of February 1944, I returned to the war at the beginning of the following month.

'In September 1944 [by which time 2.(F)/100 was based at Lublin, in eastern Poland] I lost my crew. The day that we were meant to fly, I was very ill with food poisoning. Another pilot, still a "greenhorn" with very little combat experience, took my place. Russian fighters shot them down, but he made a successful belly landing with one engine burning. The pilot got out of the aircraft and ran into a thicket of bushes and trees, where he went into hiding. He observed that two other crewmembers got out and were trying to get a third member out, but then the entire aircraft started burning and thick smoke obscured his vision. He could not see any of the crew anymore and did not know if any of them got away.

'An old-fashioned Russian biplane touched down in a nearby field and Russian soldiers and peasants soon showed up at the crash site, so he had to abandon his observation point and move deeper into the thicket, where he was able to hide until nightfall.

'He heard a terrific explosion when the aircraft eventually blew up and black smoke drifted towards where he was hiding. At that time, his biggest problem was fighting an almost unbearable urge to cough! Moving at night only and hiding up during the day, evading human settlements and living on berries and stolen fruit only, he eventually made his way through Russian frontlines and reached those of the Hungarian forces.

'At that time, Hungary was still our ally, but there he was almost executed because the Hungarians didn't know or speak German and he didn't know the Hungarian language. They first thought he was a Russian soldier or spy. He was lucky, however, being captured, put under guard and taken to the Hungarian Command Headquarters, where he was at last able to establish his identity because someone there spoke German. So, many weeks later, he was able to return to our *Staffel* and tell us about his odyssey. We never heard anything about the fate of my comrades and friends Herbert Lengwenus, navigator, Siegfried Weigel, radio operator/gunner, and Erwin Brand, flight engineer/gunner.'

From mid-1944 Ju 188E-1s and F-1s were also used to undertake occasional reconnaissance sorties aimed at monitoring Allied shipping movements ahead of the anticipated invasion of France. *Wekusta* 51, based at Toussus-le-Buc in north-central France, took delivery of its first Ju 188F-1 in June. The aircraft joined its Ju 88s and Me 410s in carrying out meteorological reconnaissance, while the same variant was on the strength of 3.(F)/122 at Soesterberg from early 1944. Its Ju 188F-1s undertook night reconnaissance of the North Sea and, on a very few occasions, eastern England. The *Staffel* lost Ju 188F-1 Wk-Nr 280197 when it was shot down over the sea on 10 May. 6.(F)/123 at Cormeilles, in Normandy, which performed radar signals collecting and communications intelligence flights, also had both variants of Ju 188.

The dangers facing reconnaissance crews in the West were no less than those endured by their bomber crew comrades. An example of this took place on the night of 20–21 June 1944 when 1.(F)/120 based at Stavanger-Sola, in Norway, sent out one of its Ju 188F-1s to conduct a reconnaissance of airfields and naval anchorages from the River Tyne to the Isle of Skye. Wk-Nr 280608 A6+HH, flown by Feldwebel Friedrich Schanze, was fitted with one 50 cm x 30 cm and one 30 cm x 30 cm cameras.

At around 0115 hrs, while over Moray, in Scotland, the aircraft hit the top of a hill some 1200 ft high and crashed into a peat bog. The four-man crew were killed. Although the wreckage was scattered, maps were recovered marked with the locations of naval W/T beacons off the Scottish coast and, on a separate card, their frequencies, as well as those of some of the main Allied broadcasting stations. Another paper fragment contained an order to crews to report any enemy aircraft sighted within 50 km of the Norwegian coast.

A few nights later, on 23–24 June, another lone mission to England was flown by Leutnant Hans-Georg Kasper and his crew in Ju 188D-2 F6+IL of 3.(F)/122 from the *Staffel's* base at Soesterberg. The Junkers took off at around 2100 hrs on a shipping reconnaissance mission and headed across the North Sea, flying at between 5000–6000 m above eight-tenths cloud. Unfortunately for Kasper, a little earlier a Mosquito flown by Wg Cdr Cathcart Wight-Boycott and his navigator/radar operator, Flt Lt D M Reid, of No 25 Sqn had taken off from Coltishall, in Norfolk, on a practice interception.

Shortly after getting airborne, Wight-Boycott was advised that a 'bandit' was approaching from about 50 miles east at 22,000 ft. Under guidance, the Mosquito climbed to that altitude and Reid took control of the

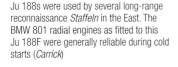

Ju 188s were used by several long-range reconnaissance *Staffeln* in the East. The BMW 801 radial engines as fitted to this Ju 188F were generally reliable during cold starts (*Carrick*)

interception. The 'bandit' – Kasper's Ju 188 – did not appear to take any evasive action and continued to climb, at one point dropping 'Window'. Wight-Boycott asked Reid to put the Ju 188 on their starboard side 'as there was a brilliant band of Northern Light in that direction'.

The Mosquito climbed to chase at full throttle and began to overtake the Ju 188 very slowly, eventually obtaining a visual in the darkness above the Northern Light. Wight-Boycott closed in to port and below to within 700 ft, and Reid identified the enemy aircraft as either a Ju 88 or Ju 188. Wight-Boycott reported;

'I then closed in behind to 600 ft and fired a one-second burst from dead astern. Strikes were observed all over the fuselage and a red glow appeared in the cockpit. I closed in again to about 400 ft and fired a one-second burst with unobserved results. A further two bursts of one-second each, fired from dead astern, produced more strikes on the fuselage, and the enemy aircraft caught fire, turned to port and dived gently down. I watched the enemy aircraft continue to dive down enveloped in flames until it crashed on land. The enemy aircraft burned on the ground for some time and lit up a wide area.'

As the Mosquito made its attack, one member of the Junkers' crew, gunner Unteroffizier Willi Scheel, was reported by British Air Intelligence to have been 'thrown out of the aircraft'. He survived, slightly injured, and was captured, but his comrades, comprising Kasper, the observer Oberleutnant Günther Hupka, radio operator Unteroffizier Bernhard Morweisen and the other gunner, Obergefreiter Peter Verkhausen, were killed when their Ju 188 crashed at 0020 hrs at Padley Water, half a mile east of Chillesford, near Woodbridge in Suffolk.

Scheel had joined 3.(F)/122 in April 1943, but had only recently become a part of Kasper's crew following the unit's conversion to the Ju 188. He had 58 missions to his credit, and his interrogators described his morale as 'low – he is resigned to the inevitable defeat of Germany'.

Still using the Ju 188 in mid-1944 in the east was the *Versuchsverband OKL*, as the original *Versuchsstelle für Höhenfluge* had become known from May of that year. Oberleutnant Werner Muffey was assigned to the *Versuchsverband* in 1943 at Oranienburg. He was known as a very capable pilot, and was thus tasked with testing many types of aircraft and assigned missions that other pilots seemed reluctant to fly. Post-war, Muffey recalled flying the Ju 188 operationally;

'I was given a Ju 188 (or Ju 88B as we used to call it), equipped with GM-1, for reconnaissance of the northern sector of the Eastern Front. Flying from Riga, in Latvia, we made a couple of reconnaissance sorties from there towards Leningrad and Moscow, then we were transferred to Thorn [in Poland] and enjoyed rather long and trouble-free photo-flights thanks to our GM-1 which, after switching it on, say, at 8000 m, let us escape any Russian fighter attacks. The only concern was, of course, the supply of liquid oxygen, which was by no means readily available. Flying via Baranowice, we finally arrived at Debreczin, in Hungary, constantly following the shrinking German front.

'After a strafing attack by American Lightnings, our Ju 188 was left rather seriously damaged, but Willy Mensching, assisted by the local maintenance force, managed to get her flyable again, and that coincided

Wearing a mix of typical mid-/late-war flying clothing, this unidentified Ju 188 crew from either a long-range reconnaissance or meteorological unit has just returned from another flight over northern Europe. The unteroffizier at right holds two briefcases that probably contain flight maps and orders (*Carrick*)

with a radio message from Oranienburg telling us to come home immediately. So we stowed half a pig into the cockpit as an additional payload where five instead of the usual three people had already squeezed themselves. This must have been watched by a Lightning, which fired several bursts of tracer at us, fortunately without immediate result.

'Some moments later though, we suddenly had the cabin full of black smoke and a terrible stench, which prompted Willy to suspect the origin of the fire to be in the electrical wiring. So he cut the master switch, used an extinguisher, and within a matter of minutes we were back to half-normal, because nothing electrical worked any longer. This adventurous trip ended in a rather tricky, but safe, night landing at Breslau instead of Oranienburg.'

Another unit to suffer a Ju 188 lost as a result of strafing attacks in Hungary was the meteorological reconnaissance *Staffel Wekusta* 27 under Knight's Cross-holder Hauptmann Dr. Hans Bonath, which had a small number of F-1s assigned to it in late 1944. The unit conducted operations over southeastern Europe from bases in Yugoslavia and Hungary, and in late October 1944 *Wekusta* 27 was at Szombathely, in Hungary, close to the frontier with Austria. It was here that an F-1 was lost to Allied fighter-bombers on the ground, while another failed to return from a reconnaissance mission on 8 November. Following further losses, *Wekusta* 27 was disbanded in December and its remaining aircraft and personnel assigned to 2.(F)/11.

Aside from *Wekusta* 27, Ju 188s are listed as having been delivered to *Wekustas* 3, 6 and 51, the *Wettererkundungsstaffel* 1/O.b.d.L. and possibly other meteorological units. From the summer of 1944, *Wekusta* 51, for example, had only one or two serviceable Ju 188F-1s on strength at any one time, and used them on meteorological reconnaissance flights from Vannes and Nantes over the Bay of Biscay and eastern Atlantic. It was dangerous work as the Biscay was patrolled regularly by RAF and USAAF aircraft. One F-1, Wk-Nr 289210 4T+AH, flown by Leutnant Theobold Fischer, failed to return on 9 June after it went out to search for the crew of a Ju 88A-4 that had been shot down over the Biscay earlier that same day.

In the autumn of 1944, *Wekusta* 3, led by Oberleutnant Hans Huck (the third *Staffelkapitän* since the unit's formation at the beginning of the year), was based at Stavanger-Sola, from where its handful of Ju 88D-1s and D-2s – never more than five available machines – carried out meteorological reconnaissance over Norway, the North Sea and the Arctic Ocean. Even with such a small number of aircraft, the *Staffel* battled serviceability issues, enemy fighters and suspected sabotage; Ju 188 D7+UH, flown by Unteroffizier Weyrauch, exploded shortly after take-off from Stavanger on 11 October while still in sight of the coast. Recovered pieces of the wreckage gave the Germans reason to suspect hidden explosives. During the afternoon of 30 October, another Ju 188 (assigned the replacement code UH) flown by Feldwebel Josef Riedmeier was shot down by Mosquitos

over the Sogne Fjord after the aircraft had aborted its mission as a result
of technical problems.

As late as January 1945, Ju 188s of *Wekusta* 3 were ranging as far as the
volcanic island of Jan Mayen, in the Arctic Ocean. On 14 January, Ju 188
4B+B, flown by Oberleutnant Georg Obermeier, took off from Ørlandet
on a flight of more than eight hours to the island. On the return leg, bad
weather and a shortage of fuel forced the crew to make an emergency
landing on the island of Leka off the Norwegian coast between Rørvik
and Kvaløya. The Junkers caught fire on impact with the rocky terrain,
although the crew was able to exit the aircraft by releasing the upper
cockpit glazed section. They were given shelter by a German observation
post and collected by the Kriegsmarine the next day.

Following Germany's surrender in May 1945, at least one of *Wekusta* 3's
Ju 188s, flown by Unteroffizier Werner Maurer, is reported to have assisted
in the evacuation of Wehrmacht troops from Kurland. During this
extraordinary flight, the aircraft routed from Trondheim, across Norway,
Sweden and the Baltic to Libau, in Latvia. Here, the Junkers somehow
managed to refuel, then take off, very overloaded, with its crew and 13
rescued soldiers and head for Hamburg.

TORPEDO-BOMBER

Commencing in the first half of 1942, the Ju 88 was outfitted to carry
torpedoes as the Ju 88A-4 LT (*Luft Torpedo* – aerial torpedo) sub-variant.
In this role, between 1942 and 1944, Ju 88s of III./KG 26 and I. and
III./KG 77 saw considerable and successful service against Allied shipping
and convoys off North Africa and elsewhere in the Mediterranean, as well
as in the Arctic.

With the introduction of the Jumo 213, it was a logical choice to adapt
the Ju 188 into a torpedo-carrier as the A-3 variant, with some examples
being fitted with FuG 200 *Hohentwiel* ship-search radar (see Chapter Two).
An underwing PVC torpedo rack was fitted inboard of each engine and a
dedicated torpedo sight installed in the cockpit from which it was possible
to input the torpedo run control settings. The racks, which were larger and
deeper than ETC bomb racks, were able to carry one LT F5b torpedo each.

Powered by compressed air, the
five-metre-long LT F5b weighed
765 kg (250 kg of which was the
explosive charge) and required
a minimum depth of water of
16–20 m. With a range of 3000 m,
the LT F5b had a top speed of
33 knots. The torpedo's gyro would
start to run as it was launched from
the carrier aircraft, and the engine
was started by the pressure from
the water pushing back a flap as it
became submerged.

The introduction of only limited
numbers of Ju 188A-3s into service

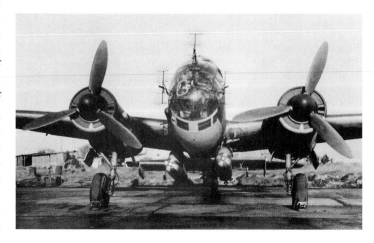

A relatively rare Ju 188A-3, which was
essentially a Jumo-engined bomber
modified for torpedo-bombing work. This
aircraft has been fitted with an antenna
array for FuG 200 Hohentwiel ship-search
radar, and it carries a pair of LT F5b
practice torpedoes attached to L 10
glide-torpedo carriers. Manufactured by
Blohm und Voss, the L 10 enabled an
aircraft to launch a torpedo from a greater
height and range, allowing it to break away
from its attack run earlier. After launch, a
small drogue would be reeled out that
released the torpedo upon impact with the
water. However, such a heavy external load
affected the Ju 188's performance
(*Hermann*)

in late 1944 meant the aircraft had little significant impact on German air-sea offensive operations. The first unit to make the switch was III./KG 26 under Major Ernst-Heinrich Thomsen. Equipped with Ju 88A-4 LTs and Ju 88A-17s, it transferred from southern France, where the *Gruppe* had been conducting anti-shipping operations over the Mediterranean since June the previous year, to Leck, in northern Germany, in mid-August to begin conversion onto the Ju 188 for aerial torpedo missions. The *Gruppe* was to hand its Ju 88s over to II./KG 26. For this new phase of its existence, command of III./KG 26 passed from Thomsen to Major Wolrad Harseim, who had previously been with III./KG 77 – another *Gruppe* that had been successfully deployed on anti-shipping work.

Conversion was completed in November, and the *Gruppe*, staging via Gardermoen, relocated to Trondheim-Vaernes, in Norway. Such was the remoteness of their new base that while the groundcrew took quarters in wooden barracks around the airfield, the aircrew found accommodation in farms and houses scattered in the immediate area. From October, II./KG 26 had also begun to move into Norway with its Ju 88s, with elements based at Trondheim and Banak, in the far north.

Both *Gruppen* were to conduct a new torpedo war against Allied Arctic convoys with some 50 aircraft in total, their operations to be coordinated by the *Kommandierenden General der Luftwaffe* in Oslo and the staffs of the *Fliegerführer Mitte* in Trondheim and the *Fliegerführer Lofoten* in Bardufoss. The problem was that by late 1944 the convoys were very well defended by escorts, including carriers that brought local air cover.

By 10 January 1945, III./KG 26 had 37 Ju 188s on strength, of which 32 were operationally ready. On 3 February 1945, convoy JW 64, comprised of 31 merchantmen and no fewer than 22 escorts, including two carriers, sailed from Greenock, in Scotland, bound for the Kola Inlet, in northwest Russia, under the command of Rear-Admiral Rhoderick McGrigor. The Luftwaffe spotted the convoy on the 6th and tracked it continuously using Ju 88s of 1.(F)/124 from Bardufoss.

On the 7th, with orders from Göring to focus its attacks on the carriers, 25 Ju 88s of Major Rudi Schmitt's II./KG 26 took off from Bardufoss. Meanwhile, the convoy escort's radars had picked up the approaching aircraft and McGrigor manoeuvred JW64 to place its vessels astern of the Ju 88s. When the torpedo-bombers reached the convoy, any remaining tactical initiative they had was squandered while crews hunted for the carriers. With valuable time lost, the attackers subsequently focused on the merchantmen.

By then, the shadowing aircraft, which were supposed to transmit D/F signals to the KG 26 force, had lost contact with JW 64 due to the convoy's counter-manoeuvring. The Ju 88 crews claimed six hits, but several torpedoes exploded prematurely and the attack was aborted. Three aircraft were lost, including that of the *Staffelkapitän* of 6./KG 26, Oberleutnant Rudolf Rögner.

The Ju 188s of III. *Gruppe* arrived at Bardufoss the following day and, together with II./KG 26, mounted a second strike on the 8th. It is believed that 18 Ju 188s were committed to the operation, along with 15 aircraft from II. *Gruppe*. Despite a well-planned joint attack, poor visibility and enemy defences hampered the assault. Although III./KG 26 reported sinking a freighter, no ships were in fact damaged. After the attack, III./KG 26 remained at Bardufoss for some time.

On 22 February, crews from III./KG 26 joined II. *Gruppe* in mounting an attack by 25 aircraft on convoy RA 64, which comprised 33 merchantmen and 26 escorts that had sailed from the Kola Inlet on the 17th. The German crews claimed hits, but again there were no losses or damage among the convoy.

In a second attack during the afternoon of the 23rd, the *Staffelkapitän* of 8./KG 26, Hauptmann Walter Prinz, and his crew sank what was probably the last victim of the German *Torpedoflieger* during the war. Having delivered its cargo of a locomotive and other lend-lease supplies, the 7177-ton US Liberty ship SS *Henry Bacon* was in ballast for the return sailing to Scotland. The ship had a crew of 40 and a Naval Armed Guard of 26 men who manned the four-inch gun on the stern, the three-inch gun on the bow and eight 20 mm Bofors anti-aircraft guns.

Having suffered storm damage to its steering gear on the 22nd, *Henry Bacon* was alone some 70 km from the main body of the convoy and, due to confusion, heading in the opposite direction to RA 64. The vessel was also transporting 19 Norwegian refugees, which included 16 women and children.

According to one report, the Ju 88s and Ju 188s commenced flying in a circle around the ship at an altitude of just six to ten metres above the gale-driven waves. At intervals, two of the Junkers would break from the circle and attack from opposite sides of the ship. One of the torpedoes launched by Prinz and his crew hit *Henry Bacon* portside aft in the No 5 hold, detonated an after ammunition magazine and destroyed the rudder, propeller and steering motor. Despite this, no one was killed, although the ship soon began to sink.

Of the 86 people aboard *Henry Bacon*, 15 crew were lost, including the ship's captain. In addition, seven of the Naval Armed Guard were lost, including the three gunners who stayed behind to the last to defend the ship, but all of the Norwegian refugees were saved. III./KG 26 suffered the loss of two Ju 188A-3s and their crews during this mission – Hauptmann Otto Fischer of 7. *Staffel* in Wk-Nr 190604 1H+LR and Unteroffizier Günther Zierke of 8. *Staffel* in Wk-Nr 190349 1H+GS.

After the mission of 23 February, III./KG 26 returned to Trondheim. Another major attempt against a convoy was made on 29 March when the *Kommandierende General der Deutschen Luftwaffe in Norwegen* despatched 16 Ju 88s and 29 Ju 188s against merchantmen reported northeast of the Faroe Islands, but no vessels were found. One Ju 188 was posted missing and two more crashed, along with a Ju 88, for reasons that are not known. The crews of the two Ju 188s were rescued by a Do 24.

A captured Ju 188A-3 torpedo-bomber formerly of KG 26, possibly photographed at Defford, in Worcestershire, while under assessment with the Telecommunications Flying Unit on behalf of the Telecommunications Research Establishment (TRE) at nearby Malvern. The aircraft is fitted with three sections of eight-dipole and eight-reflector antennas for FuG 200 Hohentwiel ship-search radar, one for transmitting and two for receiving. The lower, transmitting antenna was fixed to a frame so that it was mounted centrally and beneath the cockpit glazing, thus providing an unobstructed view for the pilot when taking off and landing. A cartridge ejection chute on a Lafette L151/3 mount is visible inside the cockpit, but the ejection port has been faired over. Note the ETC 500/IXd rack close to the root of the port wing and the flame damper on the Jumo 213 engine (*Streetly*)

The *Sichtgerät* 200 display unit for the FuG 200 used by the observer in the cockpit of the former KG 26 Ju 188A-3 under evaluation by the TRE at Malvern. The unit was mounted next to the pilot's central instrument panel directly ahead of the control column. It was formed of a cathode ray tube with a range scale engraved vertically on its Perspex display screen. Fifteen parallel lines read from 0 to 150 km, and were adjustable for search and navigational aid, and for approach and attack. The brightness of a trace could also be adjusted (*Streetly*)

The pilot of a Ju 188F-1 from 3.(F)/33 leans out from the sliding canopy panel of his cockpit. He is wearing a pair of Nitsche and Günther shatterproof goggles (*Wadman*)

In late April, the staff of the *Kommandierenden General* in Oslo came up with the notion of sending a force of torpedo-bombers from KG 26 on an armed reconnaissance to attack shipping off the east coast of Scotland. Thus it was that during the evening of 21 April, following a briefing from a staff officer, eight Ju 188A-3s of III. *Gruppe* under the command of Hauptmann Friedrich-Wilhelm Gehring (the *Staffelkapitän* of 7. *Staffel*) took off for the 1300-km journey from Stavanger – the aircraft had transferred here from Trondheim earlier that afternoon. They were trailing ten Ju 88s from II./KG 26 that had departed Stavanger 30 minutes earlier as a 'first wave'. The mission was to search for ships between the Orkneys and the Firth of Forth, with the Ju 188s assigned to cover the sea area south of Peterhead.

However, as the Ju 188s flew west just a few hundred metres above the waves, a warning was suddenly received over the emergency radio from the first wave that they had been intercepted by a large force of enemy fighters. For the Junkers crews this was to be a calamitous encounter to say the least, for they had run into no fewer than 43 Mosquitos of RAF Coastal Command's Banff Strike Wing. The force consisted of 14 aircraft from No 143 Sqn, 12 rocket-carriers from No 235 Sqn, another eight rocket-armed aircraft from No 248 Sqn, plus two with depth charges, all of which were escorted by seven aircraft from Nos 143 and 333 Sqns. This force, led by Wg Cdr Christopher Foxley-Norris of No 143 Sqn, was on its track home from a patrol to the Skagerrak and Kattegat when it came across the Luftwaffe bombers 180 miles from base and 200 ft above the sea.

Moments later, the Ju 188s of III./KG 26 also encountered the enemy fighters. The Mosquitos went in for the kill and the sky over the North Sea was full of swirling aircraft. According to the Operations Record Book of No 248 Sqn, 'it was a one-sided attack, lasting some five minutes'. Almost immediately, Flt Lt J R Keohane and his navigator, Plt Off Fielding, shot a Ju 188 down into the sea with its starboard engine on fire, while WO Blake and his navigator WO Knifton claimed another, with a second bomber damaged. Keohane remembered that the Ju 188s were 'right down on the water'. Sqn Ldr A H Gunnis observed that 'the sea appeared full of blazing aircraft'.

III./KG 26 claimed – erroneously – two of the RAF fighters shot down before the remaining Ju 188s were able to evade by climbing into cloud, where half of the formation jettisoned their torpedoes and turned back for Norway. The other half pressed on for Scotland, but found no targets and duly returned to base.

The over-ambitious mission resulted in the loss of six crews, including that of Oberfeldwebel Herbert Kunze of 8./KG 26, a highly experienced *Torpedoflieger* and observer, and a holder of the Knight's Cross.

His Ju 188, flown by Oberfeldwebel Zimmermann, was seen to receive a hit in its port engine and wing tanks from a Mosquito, after which it crashed into the sea and exploded. There were no survivors.

A Ju 188E of an unidentified unit photographed shortly before or after a flight (note the crewman wearing his parachute). The aircraft's uppersurfaces have been painted with an intense scribble or 'wave mirror' camouflage of light grey over the base colour, this scheme being intended for over-water operations. Aircraft of II./KG 2 are known to have been finished in such schemes with similar code applications (*Carrick*)

But there was to be one last throw of the dice for the *Torpedoflieger*. On 29 April, convoy RA 66 departed the Kola Inlet with 27 merchant ships and 23 escorts bound for the Clyde. It was spotted by a German reconnaissance aircraft on 1 May, and immediately the Luftwaffe's commanders in Norway planned a torpedo strike. On the morning of the 2nd Ju 188s from III./KG 26 transferred one at a time from Trondheim to Bardufoss. Along with the Ju 88s of II. *Gruppe*, KG 26 was able to field around 50 aircraft to target the convoy. Conditions for a torpedo attack were perfect – cloud base at 200 m, good visibility and a minimum swell. The Ju 88s would take off first, followed by the faster Ju 188s, with 30 seconds between each aircraft.

However, as the bombers started to taxi out, a red 'stop' flare was fired from the control tower. Brakes were applied and engines ran down. The mission had been called off by high command. The Ju 188s of III./KG 26 once more returned to Trondheim, flying individually in bad weather. The process was not without loss, for the aircraft of Hauptmann Gehring, *Kapitän* of 7. *Staffel*, crashed in the Lavangsfjord and all four crew were killed.

Despite highly torpedo-trained crews undertaking well planned missions carried out in conjunction with reconnaissance aircraft, it was bad weather, frequently malfunctioning torpedoes and strong enemy defences that negated II. and III./KG 26's efforts against the convoys. The results of the Ju 188s in this regard can be considered, frankly, as abysmal.

COVERT OPERATIONS

Among the non-bomber roles undertaken by the Ju 188 was service with the Luftwaffe's covert and special operations *Geschwader*, KG 200, a unit about which much has been written and speculated. Established in February 1944 at Wildpark-Werder near Potsdam under Oberst i.G. Heinrich Heigl, the *Geschwader* had flown a very small number of Ju 188s with I. *Gruppe*, under the command of Major Adolf Koch, since mid-1944.

I./KG 200 had been formed from the '*Gruppe Gartenfeldt*', a specialist agent-dropping unit named after its commander, Major Edmund Gartenfeldt. 2./KG 200 numbered four semi-autonomous 'Kommandos' tasked with carrying out agent- and equipment-dropping flights usually on behalf of the *Reichssicherheitshauptamt* (Reich Main Security office) under the command of SS-Obergruppenführer Ernst Kaltenbrunner. Each *Kommando* was assigned a geographic region, with operations over the West (which spanned western Europe including Great Britain, Ireland and Iceland) being handled by *Kommando Olga*.

On 3 November 1944, Oberleutnant Peter Stahl, formerly a pilot with IV./KG 30, was ordered to Berlin-Gatow, where he was told by the newly appointed *Geschwaderkommodore*, Oberstleutnant Werner Baumbach, that he was to take command of *Kommando Olga* based at the time at Frankfurt/Main. According to Stahl, in early November 1944 the *Kommando* had around six serviceable Ju 188s on strength, plus two captured and operable B-17s. In addition to these types, by the end of the war, KG 200 operated a range of He 111s, Ju 290s, Do 24s, He 115s, Ar 196s, Ar 232s, a Ju 252, a Ju 352 and captured B-24s. This range of aircraft was necessary to fulfil the differing tasks assigned, though not surprisingly maintenance and spares proved a challenge.

I./KG 200 is believed to have dropped around 260 agents in July 1944 in the East, West, Middle East and other areas. From mid-June 1944 to the end of March 1945 the figure is reported as being around 600, including five to ten women. Most 'insertions' were made by parachute, mainly using the automatically opening type. According to an Allied intelligence report based on the interrogation of a former operations officer of KG 200, once over the drop point, 'agents were sometimes reluctant to jump, in which case they were persuaded with small quantities of alcohol or even, on the orders of Otto Skorzeny [SS-Obergruppenführer Otto Skorzeny, whose *SS-Jagdverband* 502 trained operatives], thrown out bodily'.

In instances where a small team of up to three agents was to be dropped, the Luftwaffe used 4 m x 1 m cylindrical, externally mounted, plywood *Personenabwurfgerät* (PAG – Personnel Dropping Device) containers, two of which could be fitted to bomb racks on the undersides of each wing of a Ju 188 inboard of the engine.

The PAGs were double-walled for strength, a metre in diameter and could accommodate three agents lying prone on hammocks attached to rings on the inner walls in two tiers (two on top, one in the curvature below), along with a small compartment for their luggage, equipment and any weapons. At one end, closest to the occupants' belongings and feet, the PAG was protected by a domed aluminium cap, inside of which was foam rubber padding or coiled rubber tubing intended to reduce the impact of landing, while at the other, closest to their heads, were three parachutes contained within another aluminium cap from which extended a ripcord of steel cable.

An Allied officer stands next to a plywood PAG container. Dropped over Western Europe by Ju 188s of KG 200's *Kommando Olga*, PAGs could accommodate up to three agents and limited equipment. Occupants within the PAG were able to communicate with the aircrew via a telephone link (*Beale*)

After release, a PAG would fall at a speed of five to six metres metres per second. The pilot of the Ju 188 could drop the PAG in the same way as releasing a bomb by using the release button on his control column. A loaded PAG weighed about 750 kg, and to attach it to a Junkers required the use of two large, inflatable rubber bags of the type used for aircraft salvage. These were slowly inflated with compressed air until a trailer with the PAG could manoeuvre beneath the aircraft and the container could be carefully fitted to the underside rack. As Peter Stahl has recorded;

'This by no means easy task seemed to take an endlessly long time, and I could not help feeling sorry for the three fellows inside that sealed plywood container, especially as the whole procedure could not be accomplished without quite a lot of pushing and jostling. The relative size of the PAG was particularly noticeable once it was in position under the Ju 188 – in normal tail-down attitude its rear end was only about eight inches off the ground.'

A typical nocturnal agent-dropping mission (not using a PAG) was that flown on 21 January 1945 by the crew of Fahnenjunker-Feldwebel Heinz Hauck. Hauck had served with KG 2 and 6.(F)/123 prior to being sent to the *Frontfliegersammelgruppe Quedlinburg*, where, in October 1944, he became part of a new crew that was then assigned to 4./KG 200 at Finow. Here, we were 'immediately told to keep our mouths shut about everything we learnt'. Shortly after their arrival, they were sent to Rangsdorf to collect a Ju 188, with which they returned to Finow, before flying to Frankfurt/Main in early December to join *Kommando Olga*. By this time, the *Kommando* numbered three to four Ju 188s, but it would suffer the loss of two crews on operations that same month.

Late on the night of 21 January, Hauck and his crew prepared their Ju 188E-1, A3+QD, for an agent-dropping mission over the liberated Netherlands, where they were to drop a Dutch journalist and fervent National Socialist by the name of Willem Copier, codenamed 'Cornelius', and another agent codenamed 'Beck'. Hauck, his observer, Feldwebel Max Wuttge, and gunner, Feldwebel Heinrich Hoppe, along with agent 'Beck' entered the aircraft and were then passed various items of equipment. Copier then climbed up into the cockpit, followed by the radio operator, Unteroffizier Max Großmann. However, once Großmann had positioned himself at his station, Copier had to find somewhere for himself in the lower reaches of the Junkers. According to Copier's subsequent interrogation report;

'The position of the five [sic] in the plane was finally as follows: the pilot and observer side by side in front; "Beck" behind them to the left; the gunner up above "Beck"; the W/T operator in the lower part of the plane, and Copier occupying a very cramped position near the W/T operator. There was not even a seat for him, and he gesticulated to the W/T operator, who answered him in the same way that he should hang on to a rail. In the lower part of the plane, beside the operator, was Copier's luggage – a bundle firmly done up with wire, attached to a parachute, which consisted of a case 2 ft x 1 ft and 6 ft x 9 ft, containing a W/T set and Copier's underclothes and money; an entrenching tool; his leather briefcase; and a pair of shoes.'

Yet after all this effort, one of the Ju 188's engines ran rough and there was also an equipment failure, so, frustratingly, the flight had to be terminated. A second attempt was made on the evening of the 23rd, and on this occasion the Junkers took off without trouble and headed west at 2000 m. Eventually, the Ju 188 reached the drop-point. One of the crew indicated to the two agents that they should prepare to jump, and moving the ventral machine gun to one side, he opened the access hatch. Despite a warning from Copier that the static lines for their parachutes and equipment had become entangled, both agents were pushed out of the aircraft. Copier landed, but hurt his leg in the process and then quickly surrendered. 'Beck's' body was found that night.

A while later, however, as the Ju 188 headed for home, it was shot down by a Mosquito flown by Wg Cdr James Somerville and Plt Off Alex Hardy of No 409 Sqn, RCAF. Somerville and Hardy had been returning from a patrol when they were vectored onto the lone Ju 188. The German aircraft immediately burst into flames when it took hits from the Mosquito. Hauck desperately tried to extinguish the blaze by diving steeply and then pulling up into stall turns, but another burst of fire from Somerville was sufficient to shoot off its port wingtip and send the Ju 188 diving sharply towards the ground.

The Ju 188A of Leutnant Josef Thurnhuber of KG 200's *Kommando Carmen* at Bergamo in 1944. The aircraft appears to be armed with 20 mm MG 151s in both A and B2 positions. Thurnhuber flew several agent insertion and equipment-dropping missions over Italy in Ju 188s. A highly experienced pilot, he was decorated with the Knight's Cross in March 1945 (*Beale*)

The aircraft crashed at Diest, in Belgium. All four crew managed to bail out and survive

To the south, in Italy, *Kommando Carmen* carried out similar agent-dropping missions with never more than two to three Ju 188s on strength at any one time, despite the unit having to cover the western and southern Mediterranean and North and West Africa. The *Kommando* had been established in late 1943 at Bergamo-Senate to undertake short-range agent-dropping flights using a small number of He 111s and Ju 88s. So intensive were the activities of this unit that during its early operations, *Carmen* is believed to have dropped some 400 agents in one six-week period.

Then under the command of Leutnant Otto Klingohr, it slowly took on Ju 188s from mid-1944. Klingohr was lost in his Ju 188A-2 Wk-Nr 170492 when an engine caught fire during an operational sortie on 13 August at Casaletto di Sopra, 35 km south of Bergamo. As an NCO, the highly experienced pilot Josef 'Sepp' Thurnhuber joined the *Kommando* in May 1944 when it had just two Ju 188s and a single Ju 88 on strength. Promoted to leutnant, he was appointed to take command of the unit in November after Klingohr's successor, fellow experienced long-range pilot Oberleutnant Horst Dümcke, was killed along with his crew when their Ju 188D-2 Wk-Nr 160062 A3+RD hit a high-tension line during a night practice flight and crashed near Bergamo on 19 September.

Thurnhuber had flown more than 50 agent 'insertions' into the Soviet Union, for which he and his crew all received the *Deutsches Kreuz in Gold* at Finsterwalde in April 1944. He had earlier flown He 111s with the railway attack *Staffel* 14.(*Eis*)/KG 55, with whom he had become familiar with operations deep inside enemy territory, undertaking some 130 such missions. Thurnhuber subsequently joined 1./*Versuchsverband Ob.d.L.* in Rangsdorf and then *Kommando Maria* in Minsk.

He would also fly 70 special night missions in the Ju 188 with *Carmen* from June 1944. These sorties included dropping money and gold to an *Abwehr* spy at a British headquarters in Lecce, in southern Italy, dropping a team of agents over Sardinia, a regular agent-dropping mission of Italian sailors and a female spy to Naples, and a pair of Arab agents dropped into southern France. Another hazardous flight involved dropping a reluctant agent of Egyptian origin north of Rome, Thurnhuber's slow-moving Ju 188 being attacked by three Mosquitos whilst the crew looked for the drop zone. The agent was promptly pushed out of the aircraft and Thurnhuber applied full throttle. The Mosquitos pursued the Junkers as far as the island of Elba before eventually abandoning the chase.

By late 1944, however, the supply of fuel was a factor that limited the scope of *Carmen's* operations. In December, the *Kommando* was allocated 61 cubic metres, sufficient for approximately 10-15 sorties. Nevertheless, on 29 December, a Ju 188 flew a night mission from Bergamo across to Genoa and Civitavecchia then south to Naples and Milazzo, in Sicily – a five-hour flight.

On 12 March 1945 Leutnant Thurnhuber received the Knight's Cross at Bergamo for his clandestine flying work.

CHAPTER FIVE

REACTIVE DEVELOPMENT

Away from frontline service, development work continued on the Ju 188, both in respect to its design and its capabilities. From its inception, a main concept of the Ju 188 series was to use more powerful engines and strong defensive armament combined with an ability to operate at maximum possible altitude so that series bomber and reconnaissance variants would be able to evade new generation enemy fighters. Beyond the A, D, E and F variants, it was hoped that projected new versions would fulfil this need.

These enhanced variants would also be suitable carriers for the increasingly sophisticated weapons under development in the mid-war period. Indeed, in early 1944, *Dipl.-Ing.* Max Mayer, who worked as a test pilot and specialist in unmanned missiles at the E-*Stelle* Peenemünde, and who later managed *Abt.* E2, which was concerned with missiles and rocket-propelled aircraft, is believed to have flown a standard Ju 188 on test flights that saw an Hs 298 air-to-air rocket fired from an underwing guide rail. Mayer also flew the bomber during tests with an asymmetrically slung Fi 103 flying-bomb to assess the viability of air-launching. The latter was a particularly dangerous configuration for the Ju 188 because of the resulting narrow ground clearance of just 15 cm.

Junkers drew up proposals for bomber (Ju 188G) and reconnaissance (Ju 188H) versions, and the Ju 188J-1, K-1 and L-1 designs were based on the existing production variant and would be built as, respectively,

Merseburg-built, BMW 801TJ-powered Ju 388 V8 (an L-0 prototype) Wk-Nr 300002 PG+YB, photographed in March 1944 and showing its enlarged under-fuselage bomb-bay bulge and remotely controlled twin FHL 131Z tail gun mounting. The aircraft was mainly used as an engine testbed at Rechlin (*EN Archive*)

fast nightfighter, fast bomber and fast reconnaissance machines, all with FHL 131Z tail gun mounts. A second variant group comprised the Jumo 213A-powered Ju 188S high-speed bomber and Ju 188T high-altitude reconnaissance variants that featured a redesigned 'three-man' cockpit with no upper turret and a forward fuselage with a straight underside. These were seen as lighter, faster strike/interceptor aircraft intended for, amongst other things, combatting the RAF Mosquito at high altitude.

However, before any of these variant proposals could progress, in mid-1943 they were redesignated as 'Ju 388s' to recognise that the design had changed significantly from the standard Ju 188 production aircraft. To a great extent this had become necessary because the Ju 188 had acted as an adaptable stop-gap type in the wake of the failure of the Ju 288. It was hoped that the Ju 388 would also have the benefit of being a new, fast, high-altitude aircraft built on a massed scale using major components from a type already in production.

The Ju 388J fighter was intended to counter the USAAF's B-29 Superfortress, which the Luftwaffe believed would soon be deployed to Britain, while a nightfighter version of the aircraft was to incorporate a pressurised crew area with a metal nose on which would be mounted FuG 212 Lichtenstein SN-2 radar antennas. In early 1945, the J-model was proposed with FuG 218 VR and FuG 228 Lichtenstein SN-3 radar.

Each variant had three sub-variants that would be powered by different engines – the BMW 801TJ high-altitude engine in the -1 sub-variant, the Jumo 222 in the -2, and the Jumo 213E in the -3. In daylight, a maximum speed of 621 km/h at an altitude of 11,600 m altitude over a range of 2200 km was calculated for the Ju 388J-1, while at night these performance figures were 589 km/h at 11,600 m. The daylight version was to be armed with two MK 103 or two MG 151 cannon, along with a remotely controlled FHL 131Z, while for night operations the aircraft would carry either six MG 151s (with 250 rounds per gun) mounted in two rows beneath the fuselage, with the upper row covered by flash suppressors, or two MG 15s and four MK 108s with 100 rounds per gun, or four MG 151s and two MK 103s with 100 rounds per gun.

Because the Ju 388 was seen as a high-altitude combat aircraft, dive-bombing capability had been ruled out early on in its design. Like the Ju 188s mentioned previously, the early plan for the Ju 388 was for it to be armed with a tail gun mounting and initially powered by Jumo 213 engines. However, because this powerplant was allocated to the Fw 190D fighter, it would be the turbocharged BMW 801TJ air-cooled radial that would power the Ju 388.

Production was strained, as Junkers was already committed to the manufacture of Ju 88s and Ju 188s. The first Ju 388 to

What is believed to be a Ju 388L-0 under assembly at Merseburg in mid-1944. The '266' on the port engine cowling denotes the last three digits of the engine serial number. There is another airframe under construction behind this aircraft, and wing sets can be seen elsewhere in the hangar (*EN Archive*)

be completed was L-0/V7 Wk-Nr 300001 PG+YA, built at Dessau, which completed its 40-minute maiden flight on 22 December 1943. The aircraft made a flight to 5000 m on 20 January 1944, but the test crew reported radio interference, an oil 'mist' that appeared in the cockpit at altitude and the fogging of the glass canopy panes.

The first prototype of the Ju 388K-1 was the K-1/V3, which embarked upon its maiden flight on 2 April 1944. Following completion of the pre-production K-0 run at Merseburg, series production commenced. However, the Ju 388K-1 was cancelled in September 1944 and few such bombers were completed by the time work stopped in early 1945. These aircraft had the rear gun mount and an external ventral *Bomberwanne* in which a maximum bombload of 3000 kg could be carried. With BMW engines, the K-1 had an estimated maximum speed of 610 km/h at an altitude of 11,600 m over a range of 1,770 km.

The first examples of ten BMW 801TJ-powered Ju 388L-0 high-speed reconnaissance variants were ordered by the RLM on 24 May 1943 and constructed using earlier Ju 188 components at Dessau and Merseburg, but with the new three-man pressurised cabin. A second run of ten such machines was ordered on 6 August and built at Merseburg. With BMW engines, the L-1 had a maximum speed of 620 km/h at an altitude of 11,600 m over a range of 3100 km. The daylight L variant was designed to accommodate a total of 3935 litres of fuel in six relief and auxiliary tanks to port and starboard and forward and rear.

Early production Ju 388L-1 Wk-Nr 340083 RT+KC photographed in September 1944. Seen in the background is Ju 388L-1 Wk-Nr 340084 RT+KD (*EN Archive*)

The first Ju 388L-0s were delivered to the dedicated Luftwaffe test unit *Erprobungskommando Ju 388* at Rechlin for assessment and acceptance to full operational status in August 1944. The *Erprobungskommando* had been officially established on 15 July, with an advance detachment arriving at the *Erprobungsstelle* at the end of that month. By late July there were five Ju 388s at Rechlin, although that figure had only risen to seven by the end of September. The *Kommando* was critical of the build-quality of the aircraft arriving from Junkers at Merseburg and numerous faults were identified, such as leaking lines and jamming hatches, which should have been rectified prior to leaving the factory.

Erprobungskommando Ju 388 would suffer the loss of two aircraft destroyed in air raids and a further machine damaged to 70 percent. Poor build quality and adverse weather also hampered testing. Furthermore, in early October, the briefing for the *Kommando* narrowed to focus only on the Ju 388 as a nightfighter.

Hauptmann Kurt Bonow, an experienced nightfighter pilot who had once served with NJG 100, was assigned to the unit. He recalled;

'On 2 October 1944 I was transferred with my crew and my leading mechanic from the *Stab* of NJGr 10 at Werneuchen to *Erprobungskommando Ju 388*, a high-altitude nightfighter unit based at Rechlin. The *Kommando* had, in addition to myself, two Oberleutnante and their crews. On one test

The pre-production Merseburg-built Ju 388L-0 Wk-Nr 3000291 DW+YY. Atop the pressurised cockpit is the mount for a rearward-view periscope. Also visible behind the port mainwheel door, approximately halfway along the underside of the fuselage, is the ventral fairing for the aircraft's fixed rearward-firing *Waffentropfen* MG 81Z guns. Note the aircraft was fitted with three-bladed propellers, unlike later Ju 388s, although by the time it commenced trials at Rechlin the Ju 388 also had four-bladed units (*EN Archive*)

I reached a height of 10,230 m in the Ju 388. At this altitude the flight characteristics were no longer satisfactory. We considered that these would be especially bad for a nightfighter, which would be involved in poor-weather operations. During our flights we carried no armament or ammunition. Finally, towards the end of February, the experiments with the Ju 388 were discontinued, although Professor Hertel and Junkers had done all they could to get the machine operational.'

Ultimately, *Erprobungskommando Ju 388* had to report that the Ju 388 did not offer a significant improvement over existing types, and so it was disbanded on 14 February 1945. The unit's personnel of four officers, three civilians and 85 NCOs and enlisted men were reassigned to *Erprobungskommando Do 335*, KG 76 and other units.

In late March 1944 it had been planned to deliver the first BMW 801TJ-powered Ju 388L-0s to the *Versuchsverband Ob.d.L.* as early as the following month. The unit was also told that it was to fit a Ju 388L-0 with Jumo 213E engines for testing and deployment as a long-range reconnaissance machine. Ju 388L-0 Wk-Nr 300295 DW+ZC duly arrived with 3./*Versuchsverband Ob.d.L.* in mid-August, where it was coded operationally as T9+DL and fitted with Jumos. It flew from September 1944 and made 23 flights until the aircraft crashed on 5 January 1945, but little performance data had been collected.

The Ju 188 and Ju 388 airframes were used to create a four-engined version of the Junkers which became the Ju 488. As early as 7 December 1943, Oberstleutnant Siegfried Knemeyer, the *Chef Technische Luftrüstung* in the *Abteilung Entwicklung* (Head of Air Technical Equipment, Development Department), presented the project to departmental heads.

By taking the pressurised cockpit section of a Ju 388K and the rear fuselage of a Ju 188E and connecting them with a new central fuselage section which would house additional fuel tanks, the new design emerged. Wings from a Ju 388K were attached to the new parallel-chord centre section, to which were fitted the additional two new engines, while the tail unit was taken from the Ju 288C. The resulting design was designated the Ju 488, and it was to be powered by, initially, four 1800 hp BMW 801TJ engines with more streamlined cowlings – this was revised at a later stage to four 2463 hp Jumo 222 liquid-cooled, 24-cylinder radials. Bombload was calculated at 5000 kg. Junkers received orders for the first Ju 488 V401 and V402 'flying mock-ups' in early 1944.

Work commenced on two prototypes at Toulouse, in France, but efforts were subject to sabotage by the French resistance in July 1944 before the Germans evacuated the area in August. One such aircraft had been slated for delivery to the *Versuchsverband Ob.d.L.*.

CHAPTER SIX

TARGET ENGLAND

On 26 November 1943 *Reichsmarschall* Hermann Göring invited Adolf Hitler to Insterburg, in East Prussia, which was located conveniently near to the *Führer*'s eastern headquarters at Rastenburg. In an attempt to restore his declining prestige, Göring had set up a display of some of the Luftwaffe's latest aircraft and weaponry, including prototypes of advanced jet- and rocket-powered interceptors. Hitler seemed generally indifferent to the flying display, and was more keen to know what immediate steps were being taken to retaliate against Allied bombing raids on the Reich. The following day, Göring promised Hitler that he would arrange for the Luftwaffe to carry out a major retaliatory attack on London.

On the 28th, Göring chaired a hastily convened conference of senior officers at Neuenhagen, on the eastern outskirts of Berlin. Among those in attendance was Generalmajor Peltz, who had been called from the headquarters of IX. *Fliegerkorps* in France. Göring trusted Peltz.

The *Reichsmarschall* impressed upon the assembled gathering of senior officers the need for secrecy over what he was about to say, and what he did say caught most of the attendees by surprise. Göring informed them that he wanted a new series of bombing raids planned against Great Britain, with London as the main target. There was some urgency about this, as he explained;

'I have told the *Führer* that we shall be ready in 14 days. It is absolutely necessary that we should have 300 aircraft ready for the first operation. If I can have about 100 in the second attack and early in the morning

This unidentified Ju 188A has a relatively unusual camouflage scheme of large areas of a darker colour applied to a lighter base grey. Given that the barrels of both visible 13 mm MG 131 machine guns have flash suppressors, the aircraft was probably deployed on night operations (*Carrick*)

about 150, that will come to between 550 and 600 sorties – that is what we must aim for.'

The *Führer* had also agreed to wait a further ten days should a full moon help to improve the chances of success. New types of Ju 88 'pathfinders' from the specialist *Gruppe* I./KG 66 would also be deployed, using the highly accurate *Egon* blind-bombing system to aid the main bomber streams.

After due consideration, Peltz advised Göring that Luftwaffe bombers would be capable of making two sorties in one night against London, but that three was not realistic. The *Reichsmarschall* eventually accepted this.

The following month, Göring formalised his intentions in an order dated 3 December addressed to Milch, Peltz and the commanders of *Luftflotten* 2 (based in Italy) and 3 (in France), Generalfeldmarschalle Wolfram Freiherr von Richthofen and Hugo Sperrle, respectively;

'To avenge the terror attacks by the enemy I have decided to intensify the air war over the British Isles, by means of concentrated attacks on cities and especially industrial centres and ports.'

Göring planned to strip von Richthofen of his Mediterranean bomber units – KGs 30, 54 and 76 – in order to bolster Sperrle's units in France, so that the whole force would number *Gruppen* drawn from KGs 2, 6, 30, 40, 54, 66, 76 and 100 and SKG 10, representing more than 500 aircraft comprised mainly of Ju 88s, augmented by Do 217s, Ju 188s, Me 410s, He 177s and Fw 190s. He demanded that the re-equipment and replenishment of the units assigned to take part in the operations, as well as their ground support infrastructure, move ahead as quickly as possible, and that forward airfields be made fully ready. Tactical direction of the campaign was to be placed under the command of Peltz's IX. *Fliegerkorps*, based at Le Coudray-sur-Thelle, near Beauvais in France, and that planning be conducted under the strictest secrecy.

Peltz favoured mounting low-level nocturnal strikes against British power stations, or to make such attacks in periods of bad weather, thereby ensuring

While not the instigator of the 1943–44 bombing campaigns against Britain, Generalmajor Dietrich Peltz was the executor. A highly skilled dive-bomber and bomber pilot and tactician, and a recipient of the Knight's Cross with Oakleaves and Swords, he demanded much from his aircrews and devised methods with which to determine whether they had flown all the way to a target (*EN Archive*)

that his relatively small force would create the maximum impact on the enemy's economy and show something lasting for their efforts. In his view, the Ju 188 was a good aircraft for this kind of operation, despite the fact that Göring favoured inflicting maximum disruption by high-profile, blanket bombing, for which the He 177 would be well-suited despite its problematic performance to date. But, as Werner Baumbach has written, Peltz had to yield to 'higher views'.

Despite Göring's demands, the commencement of what was christened Operation *Steinbock* (Ibex) was delayed until January while Peltz readied his aircraft and crews and ensured he had sufficient quantities of ordnance. At senior level, the overall operation was known by the English word *Capricorn*, but operations were conducted under the German *Steinbock* after the astrological sign during which the raids were to begin.

Peltz employed a policy of dispersing his force on forward airfields across France, Belgium, the Netherlands and northern Germany so as to avoid the prying eyes of Allied air reconnaissance, and by 21 January, 524 aircraft from 15 *Gruppen* were assigned to *Steinbock*, of which 462 were serviceable. Those units equipped with the Ju 188, and their respective strengths, were as follows;

II./KG 2 at Münster-Handorf, Germany, under Major Heinz Engel (circa 20)

I./KG 6 at Chièvres, Belgium, under Major Helmut Fuhrhop (circa 25)

III./KG 6 at Melsbroek, Belgium, under Major Rudolf Puchinger (Ju 88 and Ju 188 – circa 30)

I./KG 66 at Montdidier, France, under Major Hermann Schmidt (Ju 88 and Ju 188 – circa 15)

Although there had been some small-scale 'nuisance' attacks mounted against Britain in early January, mostly by Ju 88s, Me 410s and Fw 190s, *Capricorn* opened with intent on the 21st when Peltz targeted London with two waves of bombers drawn from all his units, as well as Fw 190s from I./SKG 10, under the codename Operation *Mars*. The night prior to the attack, Peltz had journeyed from his headquarters at Le Coudray-sur-Thelle south to Châteaudun, in France, where he met with crews of KGs 40 and 100. He told them that Germany faced a 'very important and strenuous' period of the war. So far the Reich had had to endure Allied raids on its cities without the ability to retaliate, but that had now changed.

Owing to the considerable diversity of aircraft deployed and their differing performances, pathfinder Ju 88s of I./KG 66 would also be used to illuminate the aiming points which lay around the area of Waterloo railway station, known to the German crews by the codename *München*. This area formed a rectangle approximately 1½ x 2¼ miles, with its corners at a point just south of Borough underground station, the northeast corner of Southwark Park, a point 500 yards south of Queens Road station and King's College Hospital. After having dropped their ordnance, the bombers were to turn and exit eastwards along the Thames Estuary.

Meanwhile, earlier on the 21st, the *Kommandeur* of II./KG 2, Major Heinz Engel, flew in a Ju 188 from his *Gruppe*'s base at Münster-Handorf to Coulommiers, in France, from where the mission to London would be flown from the southwest. The rest of the *Gruppe* would follow a few hours later, each aircraft bringing with it a member of the groundcrew. After landing, the local airfield commander handed Engel a file with secret orders detailing the forthcoming mission, which he proceeded to study. Upon the arrival of his crews, Engel then gave a briefing, informing them that they would form part of the second wave, comprising some 200 bombers in total, which would go out eight hours after the first.

II./KG 2's aircraft, which would be loaded with 50-, 500- and 1000-kg HE and incendiary bombs, would depart Coulommiers shortly after 0330 hrs, fly a course towards the French coast at St Valery en Caux at 150 m, before climbing to 6500 m, making continual defensive manoeuvres and dropping *Düppel* ('Window'). After crossing the Sussex coast, the Ju 188s would gradually descend to 3200 m on a straight route to London, where they would bomb at 0500 hrs in a left turn. They would then return directly east to Handorf, crossing the Essex coast near Southend at 800 m.

Target-marking would be carried out by I./KG 66, apparently including a Ju 188 that carried a captured British 'GEE' (hyperbolic radio navigation) system on board. Aircraft of 2./KG 66 are believed to have been fitted with 'GEE' displays, receivers and maps, as well as a replica unit made by Loewe/Opta in small numbers known as the FuG 122 Truhe I and later Truhe II. The use of 'GEE'/Truhe necessitated the inclusion of a fifth crewman, the Truhe-Beobachter, who received training at a specialist signals unit in Köthen so as to know to operate the device.

At Chièvres, Ju 188s of I./KG 6 took off in both waves carrying 50-, 70-, 500- and 1000-kg bombs. Several crews were on only their first or second sorties. One crew from 2./KG 6, typical of several, their aircraft loaded with two AB 1000 and ten SD 70 bombs, took off at 1940 hrs in the first wave, but suffered intercom problems and had to turn back halfway across the English Channel, landing at St Dizier at 2230 hrs.

Reaching London, the remaining Ju 188s encountered both anti-aircraft fire and nightfighters. Two of the latter chased the aircraft (3E+OH) of Leutnant Hans-Friedrich Lenkeit from 2./KG 6, but despite his bomber suffering engine damage, he was able to nurse the Ju 188 back to Germany, where it landed at Ahlhorn. The *Staffel* lost a Ju 188E-1 when the aircraft (3E+MK) flown by Oberleutnant Rudolf Haschke and his crew failed to return.

Five of II./KG 2's Ju 188 crews broke off from their attack prematurely, and Oberfeldwebel Karl Thiel's Wk-Nr 260316 U5+CM of 4. *Staffel* also failed to return.

Despite incendiaries landing around Westminster, and dock installations, a factory and other commercial premises in east London being hit, as well as damage being inflicted to a power station and railway lines, militarily, Operation *Mars* was an abject failure, with only 32 bombs of the 282 dropped actually falling on London. Of 245 bomb damage incidents reported by the British authorities, 201 were outside the capital, mostly in Kent, with others in Sussex and Essex. Indeed from the first wave, only 14 bombers reached the city itself, and from the second, just 13. Despite the Ju 88s of I./KG 66 dropping white marker flares along the *Leuchtpfad* ('path') to the city, the marking was poor, and adverse weather and strong enemy defences were all factors that contributed to the result, but the loss of 38 aircraft, both combat and non-combat, was cause for grave concern.

After a brief period of recuperation and bad weather, the next major attack took place on the night of 29–30 January. This time, 285 bombers reached London in one extended wave, including Ju 188s from II./KG 2 and I./KG 6, the latter's aircraft each loaded with two AB 1000 and ten Br.C 50 phosphorous HE bombs. The entire force dropped a total of 715 tons of incendiaries and 310 tons of high-explosive bombs. Hundreds of fires were reported across the city and fire damage was extensive in the Surrey Commercial Docks in East London.

Obergefreiter Erich Schiml of 2./KG 6 was a Ju 188 radio operator in Leutnant Günter Lahl's crew, and he kept a diary during the early *Steinbock* missions. Of the night of 29–30 January, he noted;

The Jumo 213 engines run up on this Ju 188 finished in a typical nocturnal camouflage scheme at around the time of the Luftwaffe's raids against England in late 1943–early 1944. The aircraft is armed with a 20 mm MG 151 cannon in the A-*Stand*, with an identical weapon in the B2 position. The pilot can be seen through the sliding window panel (*EN Archive*)

'At 1630 hrs briefing for largescale operation against London. A repetition of 21 January. Approach from Ahlhorn via beacon *Nora* marked with *Lichtspucker* [Flak star shells]. Height of attack 6000 m, over the English coast at 7000 m, nose down and evasive action. Throw out *Düppel* a little before the coast and approach nightfighters without firing. Twin-engined – white – probably Whirlwind [sic]. Fairly considerable Flak from the coast onwards and searchlights under the ten-tenths cloud at 500/1000 m. Gave no great trouble. Over London itself, unbelievably heavy Flak and searchlights.

Ju 188A U5+LL of KG 2 in flight in early 1944. It is believed that the aircraft's distinctive random uppersurface camouflage with black undersides was intended as a scheme appropriate for nocturnal winter operations during raids over the British Isles (*EN Archive*)

'Light of fires clearly visible through cloud cover. Searchlights and lamps [sic] – green, red, yellow and white. Good [target-marker] lighting provided by us over the cloud. No nightfighters over London. Saw one aircraft shot down. Our bombs in the target area at 2100 hrs. Returned flat out on the reciprocal course over the Thames Estuary, then south over Ostend, direct home, making good landing [Chièvres] as first aircraft home.'

Fourteen of Peltz's aircraft failed to return from the raid, including Ju 188E-1 Wk-Nr 260325 3E+PK flown by Unteroffizier Hans Gaffke of 2./KG 6. This was possibly the aircraft that Schiml had observed being shot down. All the crew remain missing except the observer, Unteroffizier Heinz Damaschke, whose body was later found.

On the British side, the two raids in January had resulted in the deaths of 100 Londoners, with about 200 more suffering injuries.

With February came more attacks. On the night of the 3rd–4th, another two-stage raid deploying 240 aircraft was directed at the British capital, the first wave, comprised only of light-payload Me 410s and Fw 190s, taking off between 1900–1930 hrs.

Ju 188s of II./KG 2 assembled over the *Cita* and *Nora* beacons and headed across the North Sea to London as part of the second wave, while those from I./KG 6 left Chièvres under the lead of Oberleutnant Dr. Karl von Manowarda of 1. *Staffel*. At 0030 hrs, the KG 6 crews were offered a 'first breakfast' as Obergefreiter Erich Schiml described it – 'Operational rations with real coffee'. The newly appointed *Staffelführer* of 2./KG 6, Leutnant Lenkeit, was not permitted to take part in this mission for reasons unknown, but over the 'breakfast' he wished his comrades good luck.

'At 0100 hrs we dressed ourselves up in our Channel outfits, going off at 0115 hrs for briefing. Briefing as usual', noted Schiml, who recalled the codeword for London that night being *Seeschlange* (Sea Serpent). Oberst Hans Wolter, Chief of Staff with IX. *Fliegerkorps*, described a typical 60- to 90-minute briefing during the *Steinbock* raids;

'The briefing was generally divided into the main briefing, which was conducted by the *Gruppenkommandeur*, and in which all crewmembers and the appropriate officers of the *Gruppe* staff took part, and the subsequent detailed briefings of pilots and observers carried out by the *Gruppe*

Operations Officer and the detailed briefing of the wireless operators carried out by the Signals Officer.

'The crews had already dined before the briefing began. They then appeared in flying kit at the briefing, as they usually went immediately afterwards to the aircraft in order to be ready for the take-off in good time.

'The main briefing and usually the subsequent briefing of pilots and observers [which lasted a further 30 minutes] took place as far as possible in the "England Room" [Intelligence Room], which was set up by each *Gruppe* in the summer of 1943. The wireless operators then retired into a separate room. Detailed data for the pending operation was set out in the England Room in a clearly visible manner. For example, a model of London by night, from which a faithful impression of the appearance of the city, including all illumination to be put down by the target finders, could be obtained.'

The *Gruppenkommandeur* and the Intelligence Officer would give out details of the mission, intelligence on the enemy, the crews and aircraft taking part, details of bomb loads, armament and fuel and the times of take-off, assembly and attack, navigation aids, order of take-off, counter-measures in case of an enemy intruder attack, information on target-finding operations, recognition signals, what to do if captured over England, weather and, finally, calibration of watches. Wolter also described how;

'For a smooth execution of take-off, drawing up a complete order of taxiing was of the greatest importance, especially with larger numbers of aircraft [more than 25]. It must be remembered that all movements on the ground had to take place using the least possible amount of light [danger from intruders].'

Leutnant Lahl and his crew from 2./KG 6 left the briefing in the early morning of 4 February, but then could not locate their Ju 188, 3E+CK, loaded with two AB 1000s and ten Br.C 50s, in the darkness, as Erich Schiml noted. 'We finally found her, and were the last but one to take off at 0415 hrs in foul weather'. Two of the Junkers failed to start at all, but 3E+CK headed out to the North Sea, passing the *Zange* directional searchlight at Ostend and Flak star shells over the water, to the first turning point at 4000 m.

Whilst crossing the Channel, the Ju 188 had a brush with an RAF nightfighter. 'We finally curved away from the blighter', wrote Schiml. 'Arrived at the coast – *Düppel*. Over the target at 0540 hrs. Bombs away at 0543 hrs. An astonishing amount of Flak today and a number of searchlights coming through the six–eight/tenths clouds. Many fires and explosions. Once, a fine bundle of Flak cloudbursts passed us by – damned close! With all speed out of the muck.'

I./KG 6 lost two of its Ju 188E-1s during the raid to nightfighters, with Feldwebel Herakleitos Winter and his crew from 1. *Staffel* (in Wk-Nr 260333 3E+VH) and Leutnant Bernhard Ostendorf and his crew from 3. *Staffel* (in Wk-Nr 260218 3E+CL) failing to return. II./KG 2 lost Ju 188E-1 Wk-Nr 260216 U5+KP, flown by Unteroffizier Franz Flamme of 6. *Staffel*, when it dived into Maplin Sands two miles east of Shoeburyness, in Essex, and

The crew of a Ju 188A-2 coded 'K' of KG 6 (possibly 3E+KK of 2. *Staffel*) pull on their lifejackets ahead of another 'mission', although in reality the sequence of photographs from which this is taken was most likely to be posed and/or depicting preparation for a training or ferry flight (*EN Archive*)

disintegrated. Only parts of the aircraft and the remains of Obergefreiter Werner Zwintschert, the observer, were recovered by police at low tide.

The reality was that the results of the 3–4 February raid failed to replicate the damage inflicted on 28 January, which was probably a reflection of the fact that relatively few bombers had actually released their loads over London. The attack time over the city lasted only 40 minutes. Badly hit, however, was the borough of Wimbledon, where 27 houses were destroyed, 48 seriously damaged and a further 320 left with minor damage. There were five deaths and six serious injuries. To the east, at Brentwood and Upminster, hundreds of houses and shops were damaged, and in the former location, a school suffered a serious fire. Total casualties as a result of the raid were 31 killed and 88 injured, around half of whom were in Greater London.

A few more small-scale raids mounted by Fw 190s and Me 410s took place over the coming days, but the next major mission against London was set for the night of 13–14 February. Once again, the *Gruppen* of KG 2 transferred from their bases to airfields southeast of Paris, with the Ju 188s of II./KG 2 going to Coulommiers, while the Junkers of I./KG 6 prepared for the raid at Chièvres. 'There is a balloon going up tonight', noted Erich Schiml in his diary. 'Leaving at 1645 hrs. Briefing at 1700 hrs. Operation *Seeschlange*. It is going to be a big thing again. We are flying'.

The Ju 188s of I./KG 6 left Chièvres at around 1930 hrs to attack London from 4500 m. Bombloads varied from aircraft to aircraft, some carrying one AB 1000, one SC 500 and five SC 50s, while others carried two AB 1000/1.3 ELs and ten Br.C 50s. The bombers encountered nightfighters while crossing the Channel but pressed on and were over the capital at 2100 hrs, where they were picked out by searchlights and subjected to heavy anti-aircraft fire. Nevertheless, all crews could make out the target clearly and made good strikes, observing explosions and fires. It was not a straightforward mission for the crew of 2. *Staffel's* Leutnant Günter Lahl, as his radio operator Erich Schiml recorded;

'Had to break off twice as the rev counter showed only 2400, but then it reached 2700 and we were off – the last aircraft. In consequence, we flew with 1.2 boost and made a short cut to the target. With our compass out of order, we strayed, returning home on the emergency compass and landed at the third attempt.'

None of the Ju 188 units suffered any combat losses during this raid, but Ju 188E-1 Wk-Nr 260246 Z6+AK of 2./KG 66, flown by Feldwebel Hermann Sigg, crashed at Lille on returning from London after its elevators had been damaged by anti-aircraft fire. The British reported 'about 100 long-range bombers' crossing the coast, of which only an estimated 15 were operational over London, the rest roaming across Essex, Kent and Sussex for a period of two hours. Damage and fire was negligible, with one fatality in London and seven elsewhere, plus 17 serious injuries. Just four tons of bombs hit the capital, with 157 falling in Kent and Essex, most of which were incendiaries.

Undaunted by such marginal accomplishments, but probably under pressure from the top, Peltz began to ramp up his attacks. Another raid was executed on the night of 18–19 February, in which 187 aircraft were operational including Ju 188s of I./KG 66, I./KG 6 and II./KG 2. 'Briefing at 1800 hrs – London. Four x SC 500 – just the same as last time', noted Erich Schiml of 2./KG 6.

The *Zielfinder* of KG 66, which also operated the Ju 88S, lost two Ju 188E-1s as a result of this mission. The aircraft and crew of Feldwebel Werner Köhler, flying Wk-Nr 260202 Z6+IK of 2./KG 66, was lost after it crashed at Montdidier shortly after take-off, while Wk-Nr 260189 Z6+FK, flown by Leutnant Jens Herdtle also of 2. *Staffel*, failed to return from London. The other *Gruppen* escaped without losses, but the Ju 188 of Lahl and Schiml of 2./KG 6 suffered a repeat of the starting problems at Chièvres and had to abort the mission. 'Again the revs drop to 2400 at take-off. Off to the hut by car', lamented Schiml.

The effects of this attack were more extensive. Some 120 bombers were plotted over southern England, and they left 480 fires and 180 people killed, with a further 484 seriously injured. The London borough of Wimbledon was again badly hit, with bombs falling on a nursing home for the elderly.

The bombers returned to London on the 20–21 February, and this time there were 165 of them drawn from 12 *Gruppen*. The target, as before, was an area south of the Thames from Waterloo Station to Southwark Park and south as far as Queens Road Station, and it was to be marked by red flares. The take-off times of the individual *Gruppen* were coordinated so that they would arrive over the Dutch coast shortly after one another, and thus achieve a concentrated effort, which also meant that the times of attack were calculated carefully. Bombs were to be aimed at the target-marking flares.

The man most likely to be the pilot or observer of the aircraft checks the course prior to the crew entering what is possibly 3E+KK of 2./KG 6. The aircraft's code letter has been applied to the fairing of the bombsight optics window in the *Staffel* colour, which is probably red. Note also the flame damper on the inside of the starboard Jumo 213 engine, the mounting for the 20 mm MG 151 A-*Stand* cannon, the *Kuto-Nase* around the nose, the crew access ladder and, finally, the open cockpit window panel (*EN Archive*)

Major Engel's II./KG 2 put up at least 20 Ju 188s, each carrying two AB 1000s and ten 50-kg incendiaries. Their crews were briefed to fly low over the Netherlands from Münster-Handorf to the M/F beacon at Noordwijk, and then climb over the sea to cross the Essex coast at around 5500 m, subsequently descending to attack from around 4000 m. Return to Handorf would be on the reciprocal course.

The Ju 188s of I./KG 6 would fly up from Chièvres, and the crew of Leutnant Günter Lahl was hoping for a better turn of events than their last aborted mission. As Erich Schiml described;

'Slept in the morning. Lunch. Preparations in the afternoon for a fresh sortie. Let's hope we pull it off this time. We came early to take-off and got off without incident at 1918 hrs. Came to the first control point [at] Rotterdam with searchlight cone and Flak star shells. Came correctly to the turning point – *Nora*. Then climbing. She is not too good at climbing this time, and at 5000 m she already begins to vibrate.'

Meanwhile, the 12 Ju 188s of 5./KG 2 crossed the east coast of England on course for London, and among their number was the E-1 U5+LN flown by Leutnant Ewald Bohe, which carried a crew of five, having been augmented by an extra gunner. Despite this defensive addition, things would not go well for Bohe and his crew, for as they crossed the coast they had been picked up by a Mosquito of No 25 Sqn from Coltishall flown by Plt Off J R Brockbank and his navigator/radar operator, Plt Off D McCausland.

The Mosquito had been vectored repeatedly towards the 'Bandit', and had closed in several times but had no visual on it. As Brockbank and McCausland tracked the Ju 188 in over the coast, they became illuminated by single searchlight beams through the gaps in the cloud. Aware now of the British fighter, Bohe began to corkscrew violently. The Mosquito chased the Ju 188 for approximately 25 minutes, following its exhaust glows from a distance of 600 ft at '11 o'clock' and slightly below. The fighter's crew subsequently reported;

'E/a crossed gently from port to starboard, and as it was crossing back, two short bursts were fired from ten degrees port at 300 ft with unobserved results. The range was further reduced to 75 ft and visual of Ju 188 obtained against dark sky. A further short burst was fired from dead astern, point blank at this range, between port engine and fuselage.'

At this, the Ju 188 'immediately caught fire', and the Mosquito broke to starboard to observe the results. The Junkers continued to fly straight and level for a few seconds before it went into a steep dive with pieces flying off. Brockbank and McCausland noticed an explosion as the Ju 188 entered cloud 'blazing furiously'. Bohe ordered his crew to bail out shortly before the bomber crashed in flames at Twinstead, near Halstead in Essex at 2210 hrs. The crew survived, with the exception of the observer, Oberfeldwebel Karl Rittgen, who was killed.

The remaining Ju 188s of II./KG 2 reached London, but for Leutnant Lahl's crew 'the night was just beginning', as Erich Schiml noted in his diary;

'Even at the target we were no higher than 5200 m. There may have been some icing up or some trouble caused by the heavily reduced rpm setting. The Devil's own Flak over the target. Heavy, medium and light bursts and rocket guns. No nightfighters seen. We were once again in the searchlights but got out. Fairly considerable searchlight activity. Target-marking somewhat late, but good. Bombs soon out and away. We saw them explode. Then petrol ran short. Rudi had to pump or we would not have made it. Coming through the snow clouds and snow we probably passed the airfield without seeing it.'

Lahl managed to set the Ju 188 down at Vitry. The crew climbed out of their aircraft and went to make their report to the airfield commander, and the *Kapitän* of one of V./KG 2's Me 410-equipped *Staffeln* that happened to be based there poured them all a welcome cognac. 'After making our report and drinking a few cognacs, we went off by bus to food – which was good. Broth, roast potatoes, roast meat and red cabbage, lemonade, after which we went straight to bed and slept well'.

Again it was the western districts of London that had suffered, this time Fulham, Putney and Chiswick. The bombing lasted for two hours and around 600 fires broke out, causing 216 fatalities and leaving 417 seriously injured.

There was to be no respite for airmen or Londoners. The city's docks were the target for 23–24 February, when II./KG 2 sent up about 20 Ju 188s from Coulommiers, all carrying incendiaries. Reaching London at 2335 hrs for a raid that was supposed to strike the east of

London, crews dropped a significant part of their bombload on the western counties of Surrey, Sussex and Hampshire. One Ju 188 was lost when returning to Coulommiers as a result of an encounter with a nightfighter, and another carrying Major Engel crashed at Eindhoven following engine failure on a flight from Coulommiers to Handorf. The *Gruppenkommandeur* survived, but was injured, as were three other members of the crew, while the radio operator, Unteroffizier Werner Beck, was killed.

The focus of attack shifted back to 'the Westminster area of government buildings' the following night. This was a smaller raid by less than 100 aircraft of I. and II./KG 2, III./KG 6, I./KG 66 and I./KG 100, but far fewer than this number actually got anywhere near London, suggesting the demands of the previous nights' operations had affected serviceability. Around 15 Ju 188s of II./KG 2 carrying mixed ordnance of AB 1000s, SC 500s and Br.C 50s left Coulommiers and routed via Evreux to Le Havre at 5000 m and thence on a bearing for 250 km to a turning point northwest of High Wycombe, in Buckinghamshire, which was to be marked by four red flares. From there, the Junkers flew directly to the target, where they bombed from 4000 m. They then quickly descended to 150 m for the homeward flight, crossing the English coast at Dungeness and returning to Coulommiers via Lille. Two of the *Gruppe's* aircraft failed to return.

Ten Ju 188s from I./KG 66 carrying SC 500s and 50-kg flares also went out via Le Havre from Montdidier, where they took off at three-minute intervals, flying low to the French coast. Standard procedure was to climb over the sea to cross the English coast at 7000 m or more, staging via the turning point at High Wycombe. One of the *Gruppe's* aircraft, Wk-Nr 260185 Z6+HK, arrived over the English coast near Beachy Head at 5000 m at a speed of 360 km/h. After releasing his bombs over London, the pilot, Unteroffizier Ludwig Boetsch, set course for home, but was picked up in a cone of searchlights and, despite attempting evasive action, his Ju 188 was attacked by a Mosquito of No 29 Sqn and caught fire. Boetsch instructed his crew to bail out, which they did. The aircraft crashed on a farm at Framfield in Sussex. Boetsch survived injured, but three of his crew were killed.

On the morning of the 29th, I./KG 6 lost its esteemed *Kommandeur* when Ju 188E-1 3E+AB, which Major Helmut Fuhrhop was flying from Melsbroek to Dreux, was shot down by Typhoons of No 609 Sqn at

The hangar in which Ju 188A-2 3E+HK of 2./KG 6 is parked at Melsbroek has been 'restored' to give the deceptive appearance of it being a large house or farm building. The aircraft is seen here without its powered turret. Although there is thought that this may have been removed as a speed-enhancing measure for illuminator aircraft, in this example, the turret's absence is more likely a result of maintenance and/or repair or replacement (*EN Archive*)

Saboncourt, 18 km northeast of Saint-Quentin. Fuhrhop and his six-man crew, which included two members of the groundcrew, were killed. Ju 188E-1 3E+KH, flown by Unteroffizier Wilhelm Meyer of 1./KG 6, was also attacked by the Typhoons and came down in the same vicinity with the loss of all seven men on board. Fuhrhop would be succeeded by Hauptmann Hans Thurner.

Despite questionable results, Peltz maintained the pressure into March, although from that point raids would not be repeated at the same magnitude as those in January and February. The commander of IX. *Fliegerkorps* also endeavoured to spread his net, targeting the cities of Bristol and Hull. In reality, these locations experienced little more than nuisance raids. The ready strength available to Peltz had waned as well. Of 441 bombers assigned to *Luftflotte* 3 on 20 March, only 252 were serviceable, or a factor of 57.1 per cent – significantly lower than the 89.6 per cent applicable on 20 January.

Towards the end of the *Steinbock* offensive Ju 188s of II./KG 2 carried flares to supplement those dropped by I./KG 66 if deemed necessary. For example, on the raid to London on 18–19 April, four aircraft, including U5+BN, +KN and +EN, carried six LC 50 white flares in addition to their loads of AB 1000s and Br.C 50s. They were to act as 'back-ups' for the target-marking, and were to lay their white flares under the altitudes of the red target-markers at a height of about 2000 m. There was some subterfuge to this, for according to Allied air intelligence;

'No small number of crews dropped their bombs prior to reaching the target, even when the target was properly marked, in order to avoid AA fire. In an effort to curtail this tendency, General Peltz required crewmembers to describe the flare pattern which existed over the target in order to ensure that they had been to the target. Various coloured flares, of which the bomber crews had no knowledge, were dropped onto the target by target-marking aircraft. If the crew did not report the presence of these flares upon return, the *Gruppenkommandeur* knew that they had not actually been to the target.'

However, the pyrotechnics over the target in the later raids must have made identification and interpretation difficult for crews. Gefreiter Rudi Prasse, who flew as navigator in Ju 188 U5+DP with II./KG 2, remembered the raid on Bristol on 14 May 1944;

'0045 hrs. The first flares blossom in rows over the city, lighting the targets with a dazzling white light. Over them hang the rows of green sky markers, which float down slowly. On the ground, the Flak gunners concentrate their fire on the markers in an attempt to shoot them down. But it is too late. In the city heavy bombs are now bursting and dark red fires rise into the sky.'

Peltz's efforts, whilst causing damage and loss of life in several locations, but mostly around London, did not amount to the campaign of retribution that Göring craved. The lack of accurate bombing was attributable largely to the inexperience of many of the Luftwaffe crews and shortcomings in navigation methods. By the end of May it was all over. In reflecting upon the raids, Peltz remarked that, 'The attacks on the cities were like a few drops of water on a hot stone: a bit of commotion for a short time, then the whole thing was forgotten and people carried on much as before'.

CHAPTER SEVEN

EBBING TIDE

A Ju 188E, which appears to be coded 'O', captured in flight by the camera of a crewman in an accompanying aircraft. From early 1944 onwards, flights over northwest Europe by Luftwaffe bomber aircraft were never without danger from increasing numbers of Allied day- and nightfighters (*Carrick*)

On 23 May 1944, Göring chaired a conference on aircraft production and armament attended by the Armaments Minister, Albert Speer, Generalfeldmarschall Milch and a number of senior Luftwaffe officers. Göring expressed his ire at having been duped by false promises and unrealistic delivery schedules. At one point he declared that he no longer viewed the Ju 188 'of vital importance', and that although it could be 'improved in some respects, it was neither new nor decisive and must be set aside'. Göring favoured more 'heavy' bombers and a new generation of fast and/or high-altitude bombers such as the Ju 388, the Do 335 and the Ar 234.

On 6 June 1944, Allied forces landed on the coast of Normandy, pouring 155,000 men supported by vehicles and armour onto the beaches. The air cover for what had been codenamed Operation *Overlord* was immense, with sufficient capability to fly more than 14,500 sorties within the first 24 hours.

The Luftwaffe's bomber force in the West was placed in an invidious predicament. As the *Steinbock* bombing campaign against Britain faded into history in May, the *Kampffgruppen* became largely redundant and the inevitable stripping of manpower began to come into effect in order to replenish the battered Reich defence fighter units.

Nevertheless, limited operations continued. On 14 June, OKL decided that due to the impenetrable Allied anti-aircraft, searchlight and balloon defences over the landing beaches, only high-level bombing was possible, but from high altitude just finding specific targets in the confined beachhead areas was impossible, let alone bombing them. Thus, almost simultaneously, a revised directive was issued which, aside from torpedo-bombing, would switch the bombers over to carrying out minelaying operations as a priority in order to hamper Allied shipping and prevent the landing of supplies ashore.

Aircraft from KG 6 carried out minelaying flights in the late evening of 24 June with the aim of mining the western entrance to Cherbourg harbour. As the bombers approached Cherbourg from the Channel side, Ju 188A-2 Wk-Nr 160058 3E+AL, flown by Unteroffizier Günther von Freeden of 3./KG 6 based at Melun-Villaroche, was attacked and shot down at 1000 m by a Mosquito flown by Flg Off William H Vincent and his navigator/radar operator, Flt Lt Thorpe, of No 409 Sqn, RCAF. The Ju 188, one of the first Jumo 213-engined A-2s taken on by I./KG 6, crashed into the sea.

Immediately following the Allied landings, KG 2's *Geschwaderstab* and I. *Gruppe* under Major Franz Schönberger, both of which had converted to the Ju 188 in the first half of 1944, as well as II./KG 2, commenced attacks on the enemy fleet, dropping mixed ordnance around the mouth of the River Orne. Mining operations commenced in the early hours of 9 June when a solitary Ju 188 from each of I. and II. *Gruppen* operating from Vannes, in Brittany, dropped pairs of BM 1000s off the Normandy coast. Such missions continued on every night in June from the 18th–19th. Prior to that, Ju 188s carried out target-marking sorties and bombing attacks, and hits were observed on several vessels.

Mining flights involved dropping either the 1000-kg, 2.68 m-long *Luftmine* B III with magnetic acoustic detonators or the 1000-kg *Bombenmine* 1000 parachute mine, which had a tail made of Bakelite that was designed to break up upon impact. I./KG 6 deployed both types of mines, although it was more common for the LMB III to be carried, which was intended for laying in shallow water where it could rest on the sea bed. The Ju 188s of I./KG 6 would usually release their second LMB III at an interval of five seconds after the first. Crews were instructed that they should not release a mine from below 700 m, although there was no restriction on height limit – this was left to crews' discretion. Most crews tended to release from below 2500 m and often as low as 1000 m, flying at such a height in order to avoid heavy anti-aircraft fire.

A former crewman from Hauptmann Wilhelm Traxlmayr's 1./KG 6 shot down over the mouth of the River Orne in late July told his Allied captors that the BM 1000 mines carried by his *Gruppe* 'were fitted with a particularly complicated type of fuse, and they were told that neither the Allies nor the Germans would be able to sweep them'. Both the LMB III and the BM 1000 were fitted with a special impact fuse which could be set when airborne, and strict orders were issued that in the event of an aircraft going out of control, mines were to be jettisoned armed, without consideration for the height of the aircraft or the risk posed to the crew!

Typical of such operations was that of the night of 28–29 June when aircraft from both KGs 2 and 6 were active. Some 15 bombers of the *Geschwaderstab* and I./KG 2, including Ju 188s and Do 217Ms, took off

One of the relatively few Ju 188E-1s to see service with IV./KG 6 in its 12. *Staffel*. The *Gruppe*, based successively at Bretigny and Lüneburg under the command of Major Friedrich Schallmayer, began to receive Ju 188s from the autumn of 1943, operating them alongside its Ju 88s. This machine, 3E+TW, has received a pattern of heavy mottles over a dark base colour and carries a large '59' on its tail assembly in a style often associated with training units. The double rings on its spinners are typical of KG 6 (*Author's Collection*)

from their forward operational base at Gilze-Rijen, in the Netherlands, at around 2300 hrs. Some aircraft may have suffered technical failure and were forced to abort, but it is believed that three Ju 188s from the *Stab* and three from I. *Gruppe* armed with LMB IIIs made it into France at a height of 300 m. The aircraft carried *Düppel* and were reportedly fitted with *Kettenhund* (watchdog) jamming transmitters for which the transmitter and power unit were in the rear fuselage, with two antennas beneath the aircraft's fuselage. *Kettenhund* was likely to have covered the 140–220 MHz band for use against early warning radars based in Britain.

The Ju 188s followed a course from Gilze-Rijen to Beauvais, then to an M/F beacon north of Bernay, where they climbed and turned to cross the Normandy coast at Honfleur at 1000 m. From there, the Junkers turned to fly along the coast as far as Port-en-Bessin, where they were to arrive shortly before midnight. Having sown their mines, they were to return to Honfleur and then follow a course back over the same M/F beacon to return to Gilze-Rijen via Amiens. Mines were to be dropped from a height of 800 m.

Ju 188A-2 Wk-Nr 180401 U5+FH of 1./KG 2 flown by Leutnant Roderich von der Heyde, who had joined the six crews of Hauptmann Philipp von Alemann's 1. *Staffel* from IV./KG 2, was shot down by an Allied nightfighter shortly after crossing the Normandy coast. Von der Heyde managed to keep the bomber flying despite taking hits to the wings and fuselage, but a second attack set the Ju 188 on fire with the mines still attached. The crew, which had already made three similar sorties, managed to bail out and all of them bar the flight engineer, Unteroffizier Josef Slabon, were picked up by an Allied naval vessel and taken to Britain.

The Ju 188s of I./KG 6 were also engaged in mining, although the *Gruppe* also continued to fly against land targets. When attacking the latter, usually in the Caen area, its aircraft carried two 500-kg bombs externally and five 50-kg bombs stowed internally.

The post-invasion existence of I./KG 6 is a typical example of the chaos that affected the Luftwaffe's bomber units in the West at this time. Firstly, the *Gruppe* had suffered the loss of its *Kommandeur*, Hauptmann Hans Thurner, when his Ju 188A-2 failed to return from a sortie against Allied shipping over the mouth of the River Vire on 11 June – it was awaiting the appointment of a new, permanent commander.

Secondly, since the Allied invasion, the *Gruppe* had led something of a nomadic existence while it attempted to fly missions against the enemy beachhead with an average of between 22–25 aircraft and/or crews. On the day of the landings, the unit was based at Bretigny, southwest of Paris, where it had been since March with a mix of Ju 188As and Es. Five sorties were flown against the beachhead in the week after the landings, but on the 14th Bretigny was attacked by 69 B-17s of the Eighth Air Force, which dropped 126 tons of bombs, rendering the airfield unserviceable.

In one of a sequence of photographs, groundcrew haul a trolley laden with what appears to be a 1000-kg aerial mine under the bomb-bay of aircraft 'K', a Ju 188A-2 of KG 6. The bomber has black undersides for night operations and double coloured rings on its spinners to identify its *Staffel*. Note the flash-suppressor just visible on the B1-*Stand* gun, which is in the stowed position. The photograph is believed to have been taken in August 1944, when the *Geschwader* was undertaking mining operations (*EN Archive*)

This forced a temporary move to Brussels-Melsbroek, from where one sortie was flown. Two or three days later, the *Gruppe* was ordered to return to Bretigny following urgent repairs. Two sorties were flown from there, but persistent Allied attacks made continued operations difficult. So around 17–18 June the unit moved again, this time to Melun-Villaroche. It would fly from here until September. Despite the moves and attention from Allied aircraft, I./KG 6's losses were relatively low.

Aside from mining missions, which saw the Ju 188s loaded with two BM 1000s, anti-shipping sorties or attacks on landing installations would also involve loads of two AB 1000s or AB 500 *Abwurf* containers loaded with 1- or 2-kg fragmentation bombs plus ten 50-kg HE bombs stowed internally.

On the same night (28–29 June) that KG 2's Ju 188s operated over Normandy, I./KG 6 also sortied all of its available Ju 188As – around 22–25 aircraft – along with the Ju 88As of II. *Gruppe* to mine the waters off the coast. The mission was successful, but when 3E+KK flown by Feldwebel Herbert Schmale of 2. *Staffel* turned for home after dropping its mines, the aircraft was hit by medium-calibre anti-aircraft fire from enemy ships and burst into flames. The five-man crew bailed out of the stricken Junkers, but nothing more was seen of them except for the flight engineer/gunner, 25-year-old Unteroffizier Werner Stein, who was picked up by an Allied motor launch after spending four hours in the water.

KG 6 suffered a blow on the night of 3–4 July when the Luftwaffe sent a force of 62 bombers to attack Allied landing staging areas near Octeville-sur-Mer. Among the aircraft involved was that of the *Kommandeur* of Ju 88-equipped II./KG 6, Major Johann Mader, who was flying in Ju 188A-2 Wk-Nr 180445 3E+CB borrowed from I. *Gruppe*. As Mader was returning to Bretigny, the Junkers was attacked by a nightfighter and it crashed 20 km northwest of

Evreux. Three of the crew managed to bail out, but Mader and the radio operator, Unteroffizier Ulrich Schäfer, did not survive.

Mader had been awarded the Knight's Cross on 3 September 1942 and was a veteran of the 1940 campaign in the West, during which he had flown He 111s with 4./KG 54. He later flew the Ju 88 in raids over Britain, and served in Russia, where he led 4./KG 54 while it conducted attacks on Soviet supply lines and partisans. In late 1942 Mader was transferred as a test pilot to the *Stab* of the *Kommandeur der Erprobungsstellen*, and on 12 June 1943 he was appointed *Kommandeur* of II./KG 6. On 1 November 1943 he was assigned to the *Erprobungsstaffel Ju 188*, where he learned about the new bomber, but returned to his *Gruppe* a month later. Despite commanding a Ju 88-equipped *Gruppe*, Mader's knowledge of the Ju 188 explains why he was flying one on 3 July.

Three days after Mader's loss, in Germany, at a meeting of the *Jägerstab* (a committee comprised of industrialists and representatives of the RLM which had been set up in February tasked with regenerating Germany's bomb-stricken fighter production), *Hauptdienstleiter Dipl.-Ing.* Karl-Otto Saur announced that, 'The Ju 188 will be taken out of production altogether. Output of the bomber versions must first be increased from 26 this month to 68 and then reduced through 62, 59, 53, 43 and 38, and finally wound up. This type will be replaced by the Ju 388'.

However, although the die was cast for the Ju 188 in terms of future development and production, as a warplane, it flew on, all be it in more limited numbers. In early July, II./KG 2, under the leadership of its new *Kommandeur*, Hauptmann Hermann Schröter, underwent conversion to the Do 217 at Achmer, and eventually the *Geschwader* would be equipped entirely with the Dornier. However, I./KG 6, under Major Karl-August von der Fecht, at Melun-Villaroche retained the Ju 188, as did II./KG 6 under Major Rudolf Puchinger at Ahlhorn, both *Gruppen* continuing to operate over France and the Western Front.

By the autumn of 1944, the Ju 188 was still being used to undertake reconnaissance on the outer reaches of the Reich, or over territory which the aircraft could still reach. For example, 3.(F)/33 based in Greece is believed to have had four Ju 188s (two D-2s and two F-1s) on strength in October. At 1045 hrs on the 22nd, it despatched Ju 188D-2 8H+AL, flown by Unteroffizier Gerhard Eckert, from Sedes, east of Thessaloniki in Greece, on a photographic reconnaissance of the roads between Athens and Larissa, followed by a shipping reconnaissance as far south as Crete. The latter stage of the mission was intended to photograph any Allied vessels that might be located at the approaches to the Dardanelles, as the German High Command had concerns about possible Soviet troop concentrations on the Bulgarian side of the Turkish–Bulgarian border. The Junkers was fitted with long-range tanks in order to fulfil its mission.

Unfortunately, at 1245 hrs, while at 7500 m between Eleusis and Tatoi, one of the Ju 188's engines failed. Eckert released the long-range tanks and turned back to Sedes, but as the aircraft passed over Kymi, on the island of Euboea, the faulty engine exploded and the crew bailed out. Although Eckert and his observer, Gefreiter Wolfert Krecker, fell into the hands of Greek partisans, their two comrades were killed. Eckert and Krecker were finally handed over to the British on 4 November.

This Ju 188D-2 probably belonged to one of the Scandinavian-based long-range reconnaissance *Staffeln*. Note the crates of 600-litre drop tanks stacked behind the aircraft, and the single very large-capacity tank on the ground to the right (*Hermann*)

As late as December 1944, Ju 188s were conducting reconnaissance missions from Norway to the Scottish coastline. On the 28th, for example, 1.(F)/120 despatched seven Ju 188D-2s (including Wk-Nr 230443 A6+FN) to photograph the Scapa Flow naval base. This mission was possibly connected with an audacious plan to attack the anchorage at Scapa Flow with Fw 190/Ju 88 *Mistel* composites of KG 200 under the codename *Drachenhöhle* (Dragon's Lair), the aircraft flying across the North Sea from Denmark.

Göring had ordered Oberst Baumbach, the *Kommodore* of KG 200, to make preparations for one of the most radical and audacious operations ever to be considered by the Luftwaffe. The *Reichsmarschall* hankered back to a target which he had dreamed of attacking en masse at the outbreak of war. At the time his plan had been rejected by Hitler, who feared retaliatory attacks on the Reich as a consequence, but with the *Mistel* he had the opportunity to fulfil his ambition. Throughout the latter half of 1944, the aircraft carriers and battleships of the Royal Navy's Home Fleet regularly passed in and out of Scapa Flow.

Thus, on 26 December 1944, Ju 188 A6+FN took off from its base at Eggemoen, 43 km northwest of Oslo, and flew to Lista, from where the mission would be flown once weather conditions were favourable. The next day, the crew, led by observer Oberleutnant Werner Neugebauer (a veteran of 74 missions on the Eastern Front) and with pilot Unteroffizier Werner Grundmann, was informed that it should fly to Stavanger-Sola and be ready to commence the flight from that base instead. It had arrived at Stavanger in August 1944, and to the end of November had made five flights, but none so far over enemy territory.

At about midday on 28 December (the day after arriving at Stavanger), the crew was informed that the weather forecast was good. At 1300 hrs Grundmann, Neugebauer and the radio operator, Unteroffizier Heinrich Kostner, were given a short and hurried briefing by the *Staffelkapitän*, Major Schmidt. Then, at 1430 hrs, the Ju 188 took off carrying a full load of 4700 litres of fuel, 1800 litres of which was in two jettisonable wing tanks. The aircraft had sufficient fuel for around five-and-a-half hours of flying.

The Ju 188 headed out across the North Sea, the crew planning to fly north of the Shetland Islands and then head due south, approaching Scapa

Flow from the west. Unfortunately, navigation problems arose en route and the target could not be located. After searching for some 20 minutes, with visibility at 10–15 km, the left Jumo engine caught fire. With the aircraft losing fuel, the crew were told to bail out. The Ju 188 crashed into Little Loch Broom to the south of Ullapool, on the western coast of Ross-hire, at about 1800 hrs. Grundmann and Kostner were listed as missing and Neugebauer was killed, but the gunner, Unteroffizier Heinz Josaf, was captured after spending some time wandering around until he found a house. Upon being informed of his location, he was surprised to learn that he was not in the Orkneys.

Ju 188s continued to be sent out on reconnaissance by the *Kommandierende General der Deutschen Luftwaffe in Norwegen*, and in March 1945 they conducted occasional weather sorties as far as the Faroe Islands and Jan Mayen, as well as reconnaissance of Allied convoys and patrols of the Norwegian coast between Lista and Bergen.

On 25 January 1945, as Soviet forces pressed ever westwards towards the heartland of the Reich from the east, at Rechlin the office of the *Kommandeur der Erprobungsstellen* took the initiative to prepare to assemble all operationally ready aircraft, including Ju 188s, and combat-capable crews into a *Gefechtsverband* (combat unit) with which to engage the Russians if necessary. By 9 February, on paper, the *Gefechtsverband* could muster 82 aircraft, including 17 Ju 88s and Ju 188s.

Upper Silesia had been lost by the end of February, and in East Prussia, German forces were being worn down. Although it seemed nothing could stop the 'Red tide', the Luftwaffe was told that the priority was to prevent the Soviets from crossing the River Oder – one of the last great natural defensive lines in the East. Hitler was convinced that his senior and regional military commanders had so far failed him in the defence of the Third Reich, so he took matters into his own hands and appointed Oberst Baumbach 'Plenipotentiary for Operations against the Oder and Neisse bridgeheads'.

Two US servicemen examine the wreckage of Ju 188D-2 Wk-Nr 260541, which force-landed behind American lines in the autumn of 1944. The exact story behind the crash of this aircraft is not clear. Some sources state that the aircraft was assigned to KG 200, but others relay a more curious story involving a German pilot of Jewish descent who defected with the newly completed bomber, but who was shot down by American anti-aircraft fire over the France–Luxembourg border area on 29 October 1944. The caption on the back of a news agency print from early November 1944 depicting this aircraft and event states the 'Jewish-German civilian mechanic' escaped from a forced labour camp near Leipzig and flew 400 miles before crash-landing behind American lines (*Carrick*)

In this capacity, at the beginning of March, Baumbach pulled together a force of *Mistel* composite bombers from 6./KG 200, which, with their colossal warheads, would be the ideal aircraft to attack the bridges. But as *Zielfinder* for the *Mistel*, Baumbach called upon the Ju 188s from 5./KG 200. Oberst Joachim Helbig had been appointed by Baumbach to establish *Gefechtsverband Helbig*, subordinate to KG 200 and charged with coordinating the attacks.

On 8 March, in one of the first major operations, *Gefechtsverband Helbig* deployed four *Mistel* to target the pontoon bridges and rope ferries at Göritz. Two Ju 88s and five Ju 188s, all from II./KG 200, were also involved, the aircraft carrying AB 500 weapons containers loaded with SD 1 bombs. The formation took off between 0900 and 0920 hrs, maintaining radio silence, and the first *Mistel* was over the bridges between 1000 and 1012 hrs.

The low cloud base at 3000 m prevented a surprise attack, and the Ju 88s and Ju 188s had to approach simultaneously with the *Mistel*, making a gliding approach run from 3000 m down to 800 m, bombing anti-aircraft batteries around the target to enable a safe run in for the composites. One Ju 188 crewed by Obergefreiter Flakner and Unteroffizier Post was shot down by anti-aircraft fire. A *Mistel* narrowly missed the south bridge at 1006 hrs and hit the west bank of the river between the two bridges, leaving a large crater and destroying the north bridge. Ju 188A-2 Wk-Nr 180447 of II./KG 200 was also damaged by anti-aircraft fire near Fürstenwalde, but no further details are known.

On 24 March, II./KG 200 reported nine Ju 188A/Es on strength, of which eight were serviceable. Seven days later, six *Mistel* S1s from 6./KG 200 took off from Burg at around 0730 hrs to attack the railway bridge at Steinau, some 300 km to the east of their airfield. Total radio silence was observed. Two Ju 88s and two Ju 188s from 5./KG 200 flew as *Zielfinder* and long-range escort, their crews having been briefed to conduct diversionary attacks against both the bridge and Steinau railway station using eight SD 1000 and 30 SD 70 bombs.

One Ju 188 flew ten minutes ahead of the main formation, and upon reaching Schweidnitz airfield fired a recognition flare as the signal for the waiting Bf 109 escort fighters from JG 52 to take off. Once the Bf 109s had assembled, the fighter leader waggled his wings as the signal for the formation to proceed. Three *Schwärme* of Messerschmitts covered the *Mistel* and three *Schwärme* escorted the Junkers of 5./KG 200.

As the pilots of 6./KG 200 launched their Ju 88 lower components against the bridge, the Ju 88s and Ju 188s inflicted 'serious damage' to Steinau railway station and scored hits on the western bridgehead and the eastern exit to the station.

During the evening of 11 April, *Mistel* from II./KG 200 attacked the Autobahn bridges over the Queis and Bober rivers. One *Mistel* was shot down, but its Fw 190 upper component escaped. The results of the mission are not known. On this occasion, the composites were again provided with a fighter escort and guided to their targets by Ju 188 bomb-carrying pathfinders. The latter came from I./KG 66, this *Zielfinder* unit playing an invaluable role in not only guiding the composites but also acting as both escort and ground attack support by strafing and suppressing enemy anti-aircraft artillery batteries around the target. It was usual for the *Zielfinder* to fly at the same height and three to four kilometres ahead of the *Mistel*, with one aircraft acting as a guide for between two and four composites.

By April 1945, 24-year-old Leutnant Hans Altrogge was *Staffelkapitän* of 1./KG 66, now acting under the direction of *Gefechtsverband Helbig*. As mentioned in Chapter Three, Altrogge had flown the Do 217, Ju 88S and Ju 188 on bombing and pathfinding operations over England and the Western Front in 1943–44. Very experienced in nocturnal illumination and radio-jamming operations, he recalled flying as a '*Lotse für Mistel*' (Guide for *Mistel*) during operations against the bridges in the final weeks of the war in Europe;

'I did 25 illuminator missions over the London area, and most of our operations were conducted, out of preference, at night. Our targets were quite clear, but tactics were left to us. The *Mistel* operations, however, were usually attempted in daylight or at dusk from Peenemünde. The risk here was definitely greater as we navigated the *Mistel* in sight of the ground. The *Mistel* remained at sight distance. Flying height, according to the objective of the mission, ranged between 300 and 3000 m. We signalled when and where to separate the Ju 88 "missile".

'The *Mistel* pilots ran a high risk from the start on account of their restricted visual range. During the flight they were effectively fixed in motion. Once released, however, they could move considerably more easily and faster than we could. Therefore, they were meant to protect us as an escort on our return flight. In practice however, those boys were so relieved when they were "loose" that they just got the Hell out of it!'

During the mission on 11 April, Altrogge and his crew took off from Peenemünde at 1744 hrs, and having guided the *Mistel*, dropped eight SD 70 bombs from 3000 m on an enemy anti-aircraft artillery position south of Sagan, on the River Queis. They duly returned to Neubrandenburg at 2012 hrs. Another Ju 188 from I./KG 66, Z6+RM flown by Leutnant Ernst-Karl Fara, took off from Peenemünde exactly 30 minutes earlier and also dropped the same payload as Altrogge's aircraft.

Five days later, the Soviet First Belorussian and First Ukrainian Fronts commenced their main attacks around Küstrin. Four *Mistel* from 6./KG 200 were assigned to attack the bridges in the town. They were to be guided, once again, by Ju 188s from I./KG 66. For this operation, the *Mistel* were flown from Burg to Parchim and made ready, whilst the Ju 188 *Zielfinder* flew in from Neubrandenburg and Rostock. To the detriment of the mission planners, however, the Allied air forces chose this day (16 April) to launch largescale fighter sweeps and strafing missions against airfields throughout Germany and Czechoslovakia. The skies were teeming with Allied fighters.

Leutnant Ernst-Karl Fara of I./KG 66 was assigned to fly Ju 188 Z6+HM. He recalled events at Parchim;

'We received an order on 16 April 1945 to fly as an escort for a *Mistel* mission. Four Ju 188 crews [one as reserve] were chosen. We were one of them. Our mission was to serve as pathfinders, to get the fighter escort into position, to find and mark the target and to attack any anti-aircraft fire at the target. The *Mistel* were stationed at Parchim.

'We took off at 0925 hrs from Neubrandenburg and landed at Parchim at 0947 hrs. We were the first aircraft to land at Parchim, and we waited for our companions at the airfield. The first aircraft approached and set its right wheel down first and promptly broke it off on the runway. The pilot was able to hold the aircraft on the left wheel long enough not to cause too much damage. The runway was cleared in order to lengthen it for the mission.

'Our reserve aircraft was now out of action, and, furthermore, its crew was to have served as the lead crew. I now had to take the lead. There was a mission briefing, and each crew was assigned a specific duty.

'Take off was at 1700 hrs for the *Mistel*. We, on the other hand, took off when the situation demanded. We also had to keep the *Mistel* together once they were in the air. As soon as the *Mistel* were airborne and forming up, there was an air raid alarm. We left the immediate environs of the airfield

Leutnant Ernst-Karl Fara of I./KG 66 (seen here second from left) flew a Ju 188 'pathfinder' for the *Mistel* of 6./KG 200 during their missions against bridges over the Oder and Queis rivers in April 1945. His observer was Obergefreiter Leonhard Häussler (far left). Such missions required not only pathfinding for the *Mistel*, but also attacking Soviet anti-aircraft artillery batteries and dealing with marauding American fighters (*Karl-Ernst Fara Collection – kindly donated to the Author*)

and looked for cover. The *Mistel* continued to take off and were ordered by radio to fly to Neubrandenburg airfield, where they were to circuit and try to maintain formation until we could get there. The Flak batteries were able to keep the American fighters at a distance.

'I was at dispersal with my crew when a courier on a bicycle called for a crew from KG 66. I asked him what he wanted. One of our aircraft had to fly to Neubrandenburg to meet the *Mistel*. It was a touchy situation since American fighters were still very close to the airfield. I notified my two other crews and we returned to the field with misgivings. I told my crew that we would sell our lives as dearly as possible. The radio operator was to go in first and turn on all the main switches in the aircraft, especially the ones that operated the defensive armament. Next, the turret gunner should get in and man his cannon and search the sky. Next, I would enter the aircraft, followed by the engineer and observer.'

Fara's observer was Obergefreiter Leonhard Häussler. The entry for this day in his logbook records, 'Six Thunderbolts over the field at take-off.' Fara continues his account of their take-off;

'For take-off, I snuck between two *Mistel*, pulled up, retracted the landing gear and remained at treetop level. Carefully, I turned to the east. Suddenly, my turret gunner shouted, "A fighter is coming straight for us! Should I open fire?" I replied, "Keep him in your sights and fire only when he does. Maybe he won't see us". I placed my trust in our new "day camouflage". Because of our very low altitude, and the fact that he came out of very bright sunlight, it was almost impossible for him to see us. He turned away from us. Close by, a *Mistel* was shot down by a fighter and crashed into a farmhouse. The only thing that remained was a cloud of dust.

'Since we were flying in the opposite direction to the American bomber stream, we quickly lost sight of it. Eventually, we climbed to our operational altitude, and soon we saw a *Mistel* in front of us. I flew above the *Mistel* and took the lead. Soon, my squadronmates with the rest of the *Mistel* joined us and we headed for the target – the bridges at Küstrin. They were shrouded in mist and difficult to see when we reached them, and as a result we could not make out the effectiveness of the attack. Nevertheless, we dropped our fragmentation bombs into the anti-aircraft positions and then turned for home. On the way back, I pulled the Ju 188 up because I saw fires in front of me. Later, I realised that they were campfires, most likely from refugee columns heading west.'

During the night of 18–19 April, a formation of 26 Ju 88s and Ju 188s from unknown elements of *Gefechtsverband Helbig*, although most likely LG 1 and I./KG 66, attacked the bridgehead at Barby on the River Elbe. The results of the attack were not observed. There were no losses. A few more *Mistel* missions were guided by Ju 188s, with varying degrees of success. The *Mistel* units finally ceased operations on 7 May.

In northern Italy at the beginning of 1945 there were still around 12 Ju 188s on the strength of 4.(F) and 6.(F)/122 and *Kommando Carmen*. In February and March these aircraft carried out reconnaissance along the eastern coast of Italy, and they also photographed shipping in the Adriatic and in the Ligurian Sea between Corsica and Genoa. The *Staffel* lost two aircraft on the night of 28 February–1 March when one crash-landed at Bergamo upon returning from the Ligurian Sea and another was shot down by a Mosquito northwest of Cremona as it headed for home following a photographic run over Naples. On 8 March, during a mission to the Naples area, a Ju 188 had to break off its sortie because of unbroken cloud over the target, while on the 19th, (F)/122 sent a Junkers to cover Livorno and the Pisa–Lucca area.

On 9 April the *Luftwaffe General Italien* reported 14 Ju 188D-2s on the strength of 4.(F) and 6.(F)/122, of which 12 were serviceable. By 22 April, these two *Staffeln* listed 11 Ju 188D-2s on strength, all but one of which was serviceable. They continued to conduct intermittent reconnaissance over the Adriatic. Finally, on the morning of 2 May, an aircraft from 4.(F)/122, apparently devoid of any national markings, flew the head of the Vichy regime, Pierre Laval, out of Bolzano to Barcelona, in neutral Spain, effectively marking the end of Ju 188 operations in the theatre.

Kommando Carmen continued its irregular agent/equipment-dropping sorties, or 'special missions' as they were termed. On the night of 21–22 March the unit suffered the loss of Ju 188D-2 Wk-Nr 180444 when Hauptmann Heinz Domack and his crew went missing. A Ju 188 was reported as 'overdue' from a reconnaissance of the Ligurian Sea, having left at 2000 hrs, and it is possible that Domack's aircraft fell to the guns of a Mosquito from No 256 Sqn. In April, fuel stocks had dwindled to just 17 cubic metres, permitting only five sorties and the use of only one aircraft. The personnel of the *Kommando* eventually departed Italy for Germany.

On the Western Front, Ju 188s were deployed by *Luftwaffenkommando West* to reconnoitre the heavy fighting in the area around the enemy bridgehead over the Rhine at Remagen. Taking off at 0058 hrs on the morning of 11 March, a Junkers made a sortie over Koblenz–Trier–Schleiden–Remagen. When it returned to base at 0336 hrs, it had observed around 150 enemy vehicles. A mission to observe enemy road traffic in the Koblenz–Bingen–Kochem area by a Ju 188 of FAGr 123 on the 18th had to be aborted because of bad weather.

A Ju 188 carried out a reconnaissance of the Scheldt estuary between 1218–0150 hrs on the night of 20/21 March. Five days later, Ju 188s from 5./KG 200 accompanied five Ju 88/Fw 190 *Mistel* combinations from that *Geschwader*'s 6. *Staffel* in an attack against American pontoon bridges and troop and vehicle concentrations near Oppenheim. The operation seems to have been a failure. Ju 188A-2 Wk-Nr 180402 of 5./KG 200 suffered 20 percent damage at Burg in an emergency landing following engine failure, but whether this was upon returning from the Oppenheim mission is not known.

On 15 April, 14. *Fliegerdivision* assembled a force of 104 aircraft, comprising Fw 190s from NSGr 20 and III./KG 200 as well as 20 Ju 88s and seven Ju 188s from I./KG 66, to attack the Allied pontoon crossings over the River Aller at Rethem. I./KG 66 reported sighting three hits on the bridge, but four aircraft were damaged and another posted missing.

In the east in the spring of 1945, Ju 188s were still active carrying out reconnaissance for *Luftflottenkommando* 6. For example, on 8 March, under the tactical control of FAG 2, two Junkers of 5.(F)/122 based at Finow conducted a reconnaissance over Stargard–Königsberg–Landsberg and stretches of the Oder, while a single Ju 188 of 4.(F)/11 covered Fürstenberg–Greifenhagen. An aircraft from FAG 2's other Ju 188 unit, 2.(F)/100 at Welzow, dropped 16,000 leaflets over Guben and the besieged 'fortress' city of Breslau. The staff of the *Fliegerführer* 6 (led by Oberst Ulrich Klintzsch) based at Bad Ahlbeck, which was a tactical command of *Luftwaffenkommando* 6, also had a single Ju 188 that undertook reconnaissance of the Kronstadt area.

On 9 April, *Luftwaffenkommando* 4, covering Austria and the southeastern approaches to the Reich, listed some ten Ju 88s and Ju 188s on the strength of 3.(F)/33, as well as 12 Ju 188s with 3.(F)/121 based at Hörsching, with elements at Königgrätz, although a significant part of the *Staffel* had been captured by the Russians. This figure had been reduced to 11 by the 24th, with 11 crews.

To the north, the *Kommandierende General der Deutschen Luftwaffe in Dänemark* reported six Ju 188s, of which four were serviceable on the strength of 1.(F)/33. It was probably a Ju 188 from this *Staffel* that carried out a weather flight over the Frisian Islands from Heligoland to the northwest of Texel on 21 March, as well as a 'defensive reconnaissance' of the North Sea from Heligoland to the west of Texel between 1850–2314 hrs on the 23rd. Another flew a similar sortie of the western Skagerrak and sea area northeast

A Ju 188F-1 *Erkunder* believed to be from 1.(F)/120 based in Norway in 1944–45. Carrying nearly 5000 litres of fuel, some of which was stored in two jettisonable 600-litre tanks as seen here, it was possible for a Ju 188F-1 to make the five-and-a-half-hour return trip from Stavanger-Sola to north of the Shetland Islands, south to the Orkney Islands, passing over Scapa Flow, before heading east across the North Sea and back to Norway (*Author's Collection*) of Jutland, but this was only partially completed as the aircraft developed engine trouble. A similar attempt was made on the 27th from west of Jutland to north of the Frisian Islands.

VIII. *Fliegerkorps* reported 15 Ju 188D-2s on the strength of 3.(F)/121, with nine serviceable and 12 crews, on 23 April, along with four (one serviceable) with *Aufklärungsstaffel* 4.(F)/*Nacht*, but there were no crews to fly them.

IN SUMMATION

There was an intrinsic link between the Ju 88 and Ju 188, although the latter was, in reality, a new and 'cleaner-looking' aeroplane. Aside from the cleaner design and more aerodynamic cockpit, there was a slight increase in size and weight and an improvement in performance with the BMW 801 and Jumo 213 engines. The armament was increased significantly both in the number of weapons and their calibre, and a power-driven upper turret was fitted in many aircraft. As Ernst Zindel noted;

'The take-off weight of the Ju 88 had gradually increased from an initial 10,400 kg to over 12,000 kg, but the weight of the Ju 188 increased by a further 1500 kg mainly due to heavier armament, armour and radio equipment, which altogether weighed around 1100 kg. Accordingly, the wingspan increased from the original 18.35 m to 22 m and the size of the wing from 52.5 m² to 56.6 m².'

The increase in armament called for an increase in crew, which in turn marked awareness of enemy fighter capability. However, a weak point with the Ju 188 was that its armament could comprise three different calibres, which meant that ammunition from an unserviceable gun could not be used in the other guns and ammunition could not be changed to meet repeated attacks from a particular quadrant.

Nevertheless, despite delay and pontification from the RLM, what emerged from Junkers was an extremely capable aircraft that fulfilled the roles of day and night bomber, reconnaissance aircraft, target-finder and illuminator, torpedo-bomber, weather reconnaissance and agent insertion. Truly, a multi-role aircraft, and one which lived on into the post-war world when the French Navy utilised four Ju 188Es to trial the *'Fritz-X'* guided bomb and the Hs 293 glide-bomb in 1948–49.

A classic photograph of seven Ju 188A-3s of III./KG 26, with two of the *Geschwader*'s Ju 88s parked behind, at Gardermoen in May 1945, shortly after the cessation of hostilities. At far right is 1H+BD, followed by Wk-Nr 190608, 1H+BR of 7./KG 26, then 1H+D?. All the aircraft have been finished in individual 'wave mirror', over-water, scribble camouflage, although the absence of such a scheme on the port engines of 1H+BR and the machine at fourth from right reveal replacements. 1H+BR, flown by Feldwebel Horst Hampel, incurred ten percent damage during a landing at Trondheim on 23 February, which was the cause of the replacement. The aircraft have had their armament removed, while some have at least part of their FuG 200 antenna mountings still in place (*EN Archive*)

APPENDICES

COLOUR PLATES COMMENTARY

1

Ju 188 V1 (Ju 88 V44) Wk-Nr 1687 NF+KQ, possibly at *Erprobungsstelle* Rechlin, Germany, 1942

Wk-Nr 1687 is depicted here in the dark green RLM 70/71 splinter pattern it wore whilst undergoing flight testing. The aircraft carried a forward-firing MG 151/20 (A-*Stand*), a turret-mounted MG 131 (B2-*Stand*) and a further such rear-firing weapon in the rear cockpit (B1-*Stand*).

2

Ju 188E-0 Wk-Nr 10001 CG+CE, Junkers AG, Bernburg, Germany, spring 1943

This unarmed aircraft was also finished in a standard RLM 70/71 splinter pattern. Note the antenna mast aft of the cockpit.

3

Ju 188A-2 U5+LL of 3./KG 2, Eindhoven, the Netherlands, early 1944

This aircraft carried what is believed to have been a trial winter scheme using larger areas of a light colour, probably RLM 76, on uppersurfaces and engine nacelles, broken up by a random pattern of black lines (RLM 22). The black extended to the lower fuselage and undersides. No *Hakenkreuz* appears to have been carried by the bomber, although its omission may have been temporary. Only the last two letters of the fuselage code were prominent, and these would have been applied in the 3. *Staffel* colour of yellow with no outline.

4

Ju 188F-1 4N+FL of 3.(F)/22, northern Russia, early 1944

Comparatively few Ju 188s were deployed in the East, but this example was used for long-range reconnaissance over northern Russia. The aircraft received an overall wash of white winter paint, which was applied around the (indistinct) *Werknummer* and the *Hakenkreuz* on the fin and small unit code forward of the *Balkenkreuze*, leaving minimal areas of the original RLM 70/71 visible. The black aircraft letter 'F' was outlined in the 3. *Staffel* colour of yellow. The port engine unit appears to have been finished in a different colour, possibly RLM 74 or 75, suggesting a recent replacement.

5

Ju 188E-1 of I./KG 66, Montdidier, France, autumn 1943

Typical of aircraft which offered radio guidance for larger formations of bombers attacking targets in England in 1944, this machine was painted in a base colour of RLM 76 on its upper fuselage and wing uppersurfaces, over which a random, thin scribble of a grey, possibly RLM 74 *graugrün*, was applied. The demarcation line with the undersurface black appeared at roughly a halfway point along the side of the fuselage. National markings were outlined in a muted grey. The aircraft is depicted with KG 66's unit code of Z6 applied to the upper tail fin, as was seen on several examples of the *Gruppe*'s aircraft. The aircraft had no upper turret, possibly as a speed enhancement modification.

6

Ju 188A-2 3E+HK of 2./KG 6, Brussels-Melsbroek, Belgium, 1944

The aircraft was finished in a 'bold' scheme for nocturnal operations. The upper fuselage was in a base of RLM 76, which was broken up by stripes of black. The latter colour also covered the lower fuselage and underside of the aircraft. The uppersurface of the wings were in an identical shade of grey, but the black stripes were applied in a more irregular pattern. It is possible that the code was in grey, with the aircraft letter outlined in the *Gruppe* colour of red.

7

Ju 188A ??+RM, unit unknown, France, 1944

Understood to have been captured at Juvincourt by US forces, this aircraft was finished in a base RLM 70/71 splinter pattern, over which was applied what was probably a dense, soft and lighter green scribble of RLM 73 *grün*. From photographs of the aircraft, it would appear the scribble was more prevalent over the tail assembly, forward fuselage and upper engine nacelle areas. The aircraft letter 'R' appears to have been in red or blue, which does not conform to code practice, given the letter 'M' denotes a 4. *Staffel* machine.

8

Ju 188A-2 U5+KH of 1./KG 2, Lyon-Bron, France, 1944

This bomber had a relatively unusual scheme comprising an RLM 70/71 base over which had been applied wide areas of what is believed to have been RLM 76 *graublau*. The rudder would appear to have been a replacement part finished in RLM 70 with an RLM 76 scribble. The *Stammkennzeichen* (fuselage code letters) could have been either a dark grey or muted red. The *Werknummer* (indiscernible) can be seen at the top of the tail fin and the fuselage code lower down in white. It is possible another number appeared in a central position on the rudder. Other views of this aircraft indicate an unusual striped(?) pattern on the wing uppersurfaces. The undersides of the aircraft were almost certainly painted black.

9

Ju 188D-1 or D-2 Wk-Nr ??0579 (possibly 150579) 8H+OH of 1./Aufkl.Gr. 33, northern Germany or Denmark, April 1945

This aircraft was possibly adorned with RLM 76 painted or sprayed in wide stripes of scribble over a base RLM 70/71 splinter. Its aircraft letter 'O' was in the *Staffel* colour of white. The *Hakenkreuz* appears to have been retouched in a highly non-standard way, as was the *Werknummer*. The aircraft was fitted with FuG 217R aerials on the uppersurfaces of its wings.

10

Ju 188A-3 Wk-Nr 190608 1H+BR of III./KG 26, Oslo-Gardermoen, Norway, May 1945

The aircraft was fitted with FuG 200 radar (although most of the other Ju 188s from this grouping at Gardermoen had their antennas removed) and, with the exception of the port engine cowling, had an all-over meander 'scribble' pattern for over-water operations. This was applied in either RLM 76 *graublau* or possibly a duller RLM 02 *grau* over a standard RLM 70/71 *schwarzgrün/dunkelgrün* splinter base. The absence of the scribble on the engine cowling suggests a replacement part. The last four digits of the Werknummer were applied in white to the top of the tail fin, and the aircraft letter 'B' was in black, outlined in yellow.

11

Ju 188D Wk-Nr (???)133 F2+SM possibly of 4./Erg.FAGr 4, Braunschweig area, Germany, April–May 1945

Photographic evidence points to this aircraft being finished in one, darker colour, possibly RLM 70 or 72, from the forward fuselage along to a point aft of the fuselage code. From that point, following a hard vertical demarcation line, the scheme appears to be RLM 70/71 splinter. By comparison, the upper fuselage from the top of the *Balkenkreuze* and the engine nacelles appear to be RLM 71. The aircraft carries the F2 code of *Ergänzungs-Fernaufklärungsgruppe* 4 (Long-Range Reconnaissance Replacement Group), while its individual letter 'S' appears to have been in either grey, blue or red, outlined in white. The rudder was adorned with the last three numbers of the *Werknummer*, which, according to recent research, may have been 133, and the letter 'S' in white. The aircraft was equipped with flame-dampers.

12

Ju 188A Wk-Nr 190339 1H+KS III./KG 26, Copenhagen-Kastrup, Denmark, 1945

Finished in a similar scribble/meander style as the III./KG 26 aircraft depicted in Profile 10, this Ju 188A had flown into Copenhagen from Kurland. The first two small letters of the aircraft code were barely discernible and the other letters were in black and not outlined. The last four digits of the *Werknummer* were applied in white to the top of the tail fin, and a further number, 5488, was visible close to the fuselage/tail unit join. The starboard engine cowling was heavily stained from exhaust. Of note, the aircraft also seemed to have a white outline *Hakenkreuz* on the starboard side of the tail and a solid black version outlined in white on the port side.

13

Ju 188E-1 Wk-Nr 200232 (or 200292?) A3+LD of 4./KG 200 (*Kommando Carmen*), northern Italy or Mühldorf, Germany, early 1945

Operated by KG 200 for agent-dropping missions, this aircraft carried a more complex, dual-colour scribble pattern probably in a mix of RLM 76 and 77 over an RLM 70/71 splinter base, with black undersides. The *Werknummer* was applied in full below the obscured *Hakenkreuz*. The aircraft code was in small letters, probably white, with the latter two spaced apart.

14

Ju 188D-1(?) Wk-Nr 230424 9A+LM, unit unknown, US zone of operations, May 1945

This aircraft's fuselage unit code was possibly 9A, which presents something of a mystery. The last letter of the code was 'M', denoting 4. *Staffel*. While the aircraft code letter 'L' appeared in a darker colour, possibly red, the outline was in strong white, conforming to 4. *Staffel*. The *Werknummer* was applied in an unusual configuration.

15

Ju 188A-3 Wk-Nr 190336 1H+BS of III./KG 26, Oslo-Gardermoen, Norway, May 1945

This aircraft was also finished in a similar scribble/meander style as the III./KG 26 aircraft depicted in Profile 10. In the well-known photograph of Wk-Nr 190336 it has no FuG 200 antennas fitted, or they had been removed, but mountings were installed, and so it is shown here in full operational configuration. The four-digit *Werknummer* on the tail fin was partially obscured by the RLM 76 *graublau* meander.

16

Ju 188D-2 7A+MM of 4.(F)/121, Hradec-Králové, Czechoslovakia, April 1945

Among many Luftwaffe aircraft to end up within Czech territory towards the end of the war was this Ju 188 of 4.(F)/121, which must have flown there from the *Staffel*'s base at Alt-Lönnewitz. It was finished in a standard RLM 70/71 splinter pattern. The *Balkenkreuze* and aircraft code was stained and the Ju 188 was armed with an MG 131 rather than an MG 151 in A-*Stand*.

17

Ju 188A Wk-Nr 0316 1H+FT of III./KG 26, Lübeck-Blankesee, Germany, May 1945

Wk-Nr 0316 was similar in finish to other III. *Gruppe* Ju 188s with random scribble. Again, the individual aircraft letter appears to have been applied in black, possibly outlined in the 9. *Staffel* colour of yellow. As well as being marked on the fin tip, the *Werknummer* was also carried just below the cockpit glazing inboard of the engines. An indiscernible four-digit number was applied just below the fuselage/tail unit join. The port side engine nacelle panel was a replacement piece.

18

Ju 188D-2 Wk-Nr 230422 K7+CK of *Aufklärungsstaffel* 2.(F)/*Nacht*, Marienlyst-Østersøbad, Denmark, May 1945

The scribble/meander pattern was adopted in variations by units flying the Ju 188 in different roles, such as on this reconnaissance machine, but the patterns commonly reflected overwater deployment. The aircraft code letter 'C' was in red, outlined in white.

19

Ju 188A-3 1H+KS of III./KG 26, Lübeck-Blankensee, Germany, May 1945

This III./KG 26 aircraft was one of three Ju 188s to fly into Blankensee from Kurland along with 11 Ju 88s. The RLM 76 *graublau* scribble camouflage appears sparser and perhaps applied in a more hurried fashion than that seen on other aircraft of the *Gruppe*. There is one curious aspect – the individual aircraft letter 'K' appears in a light colour, probably white or yellow, denoting an aircraft of 7. or 9. *Staffel*, the former shown here.

20

Ju 188A-3 Wk-Nr 190327 1H+GT formerly of III./KG 26, RAE Farnborough, England, August 1945

This aircraft's *Hakenkreuz* was painted over with a patch of lighter green, as was the rudder. A British roundel was applied over the fuselage and wing *Balkenkreuze* and the British Air Ministry code AM113 stencilled onto the rear fuselage aft of the original code. It would seem that the aircraft individual letter 'G' was in black, possibly outlined in the 9. *Staffel* colour of yellow.

21

Ju 388 V8/L-0 Wk-Nr 300002 PG+YB, Junkers AG Merseburg and *Erprobungsstelle* Rechlin, Germany, early 1944

This prototype aircraft, which was used for pre-series testing, was finished in a standard RLM 70/71 splinter pattern with RLM 65 undersides.

22

Ju 388L-0 Wk-Nr 300291 DW+YY, Junkers AG Merseburg, Germany, April–May 1944

One of the first L-0 variants to be completed at Merseburg, Wk-Nr 300291 is seen here in its initial state (when it was fitted with three-bladed propellers) before moving to Rechlin. The aircraft was probably finished in an overall RLM 75/76 blue-grey with RLM 66 dark grey on the canopy framing and RLM 70 green propeller blades. The bomber was fitted with a ventral weapons pod intended to house an MG 131Z and had an FuG 101 with trailing antenna.

23

Ju 388K-0 Wk-Nr 230151 KS+TA, Junkers AG Merseburg, Germany, May–June 1944

The first K-0 pre-production aircraft, Wk-Nr 230151 was fitted with four-bladed propellers in the spring of 1944. The aircraft probably had RLM 76 uppersurfaces, including the canopy framing and spinners, and RLM 22 black undersurfaces, with RLM 70 green propeller blades.

24

Ju 388L-1 Wk-Nr 560049, Junkers AG Merseburg, May 1945

This aircraft, built by Weserflug at Liegnitz, was captured by American forces at Merseburg and later shipped to the USA. The uppersurfaces were probably in an RLM 81/82 pattern, while the undersurfaces, fuselage sides, fin and rudder were finished in RLM 76 and 82, with spots of 81. The spinners and propeller blades were in RLM 70, the cockpit framing in RLM 66 and either RLM 75 or RLM 81/82 mottling applied over the fin and rudder's base coat.

SELECTED BIBLIOGRAPHY AND SOURCES

Archival Sources

RLM Ju 188E-1 *Flugzeug Handbuch* issued September 1943

Junkers Ju 188E-1 u. F-1 *Baubeschreibung* issued January 1943

Various British Intelligence ADI(K) reports, aircrew combat reports, Operations Record Books, MAAF Signal Intelligence Service monthly reports, Air Staff Post Hostilities Intelligence Requirement on German Air Force Bomber Operations, AHB.6 Translations

Luftwaffenkommando West situation reports

Anlagen to the *Kriegstagbuch* of the OKL, 24/11/43–26/5/44

Published Sources

Author unknown, *Brief History of the Ju 188, Archiv* Vol 2, No 8, 1967

Balke, Ulf, *Der Luftkrieg in Europe 1941–1945: Die Einsätze des Kampfgeschwaders 2 gegen England und über dem Deutschen Reich, Teil 2*, Bechtermünz Verlag, 1997

Beale, Nick, *On an Evil Journey, Aviation News*, 27/10–9/11/89

Beale, Nick, D'Amico, Ferdinando and Valentini, Gabriele, *Air War Italy 1944–45 – The Axis Air Forces from the Liberation of Rome to the Surrender*, Airlife, 1996

Beauvais, Heinrich, Kössler, Karl, Mayer, Max and Regel, Christoph, *German Secret Flight Test Centres to 1945*, Midland Publishing, 2002

Budraß, Lutz, *Flugzeugindustrie und Luftrüstung in Deutschland 1918–1945*, Droste Verlag, 1998

Gellermann, Günther W, *Moskau ruft Heeresgruppe Mitte: Was nicht im Wehrmachtbericht stand – Die Einsätze des geheimen Kampfgeschwaders 200 im Zweiten Weltkrieg*, Bernard and Graefe Verlag, 1988

Horn, Jan, *Wir flogen gen Westen: Die Chronik des Kampfgeschwaders 6 der deutschen Luftwaffe 1941–1945*, 2004

Kaiser, Jochen, *Die Ritterkreuzträger der Kampfflieger – Band 1*, Luftfahrtverlag-Start, 2010

Kaiser, Jochen, *Die Ritterkreuzträger der Kampfflieger – Band 2*, Luftfahrtverlag-Start, 2011

Kay, Antony L, *Junkers Aircraft and Engines 1913–1945*, Putnam Aeronautical Books, 2004

Kington, John A. and Selinger, Franz, *Wekusta – Luftwaffe Meteorological Reconnaissance Units and Operations 1938–1945*, Flight Recorder Publications, 2006

Meredith, Richard, *Phoenix – A Complete History of the Luftwaffe 1918–1945: Volume 2 – The Genesis of Air Power 1935–1937*, Helion and Company, 2017

Michulec, Robert, *Ju 188/Ju 388 Pt 1*, AJ Press, 1998

Michulec, Robert, *Ju 188/Ju 388 Pt 2*, AJ Press, 1998

Price, Alfred, *Target Bristol, Archiv, Vol 3, No 12*, Gruppe 66, 1969

Rawnsley, C F and Wright, Robert, *Night Fighter*, Corgi Books, London, 1969

Schmidt, Rudi, *Achtung – Torpedos los! – Der strategische und operativ Einsatz des Kampfgeschwaders 26*, Edition Dörfler, undated

Smith, J Richard, Creek, Eddie J and Petrick, Peter, *On Special Missions – The Luftwaffe's Research and Experimental Squadrons 1923–1945*, Classic Publications, 2003

Stahl, P W, *KG 200 – The True Story*, Jane's Publishing, 1981

Steenbeck, Alexander, *Die Spur des Löwen – Der Weg des Löwengeschwaders durch Europa*, 2012

Thomas, Geoffrey J and Ketley, Barry, *KG 200 – The Luftwaffe's Most Secret Unit*, Hikoki Publications, 2003

Trenkle, Fritz, *Die deutschen Funk-Navigations- und Funk-Führungsverfahren bis 1945*, Motorbuch Verlag, 1979

Vajda, Ferenc A and Dancey, Peter, *German Aircraft Industry and Production 1933–1945*, Airlife, Shrewsbury, 1998

Vernaleken, Christoph and Handig, Martin, *Junkers Ju 388 – Development, Testing and Production of the Last Junkers High-Altitude Aircraft*, Schiffer Military History, 2006

Wadman, David, *Aufklärer – Luftwaffe Reconnaissance Aircraft and Units 1935–1941, Volume One*, Classic Publications, 2007

Wadman, David, *Aufklärer – Luftwaffe Reconnaissance Aircraft and Units 1942–1945, Volume Two*, Classic Publications, 2007

Wagner, Wolfgang, *Hugo Junkers – Pionier der Luftfahrt – seine Flugzeuge*, Bernard & Graefe, Bonn, 1996

Zindel, Ernst, *Die Geschichte und Entwicklung des Junkers-Flugzeugbaus von 1910 bis 1945 und bis zum endgültigen Ende 1970*, Deutsche Gesellschaft für Luft- und Raumfahrt, 1979

Website Sources

Aircrew Remembrance Society3 at https://luftwaffelosses.com

www.convoyweb.org.uk/ra/index.html

Beale, Nick, *Kdo.Olga and Agent Cornelius: 23 January 1945* at www.ghostbombers.com/Olga/olga1.html

Invasion watch: 18 April–5 June 1944 at www.ghostbombers.com/recon/Watch/intro.html

The Ketteunhund radar jammer at http://www.ghostbombers.com/kf4/West/kettenhund.html

H-041-1: Forgotten Valor—LTJG Sippola and the Ordeal of the SS Henry Bacon, 23 February 1945 at www.history.navy.mil/about-us/leadership/director/directors-corner/h-grams/h-gram-041/h-041-1.html

Michael Holm's site *The Luftwaffe 1933–1945* at www.ww2.dk

The Hugo Junkers Homepage at http://hugojunkers.bplaced.net/index.html

Acknowledgements

My immediate thanks to Andy Saunders. In the wake of some of my own pertinent documents being lent some years ago, never to be returned, and because, for many months, I was unable to access closed official archives in order to research and locate new copies of said documents, Andy very kindly and very quickly answered my call and came to my aid with his own copies.

As ever, I must recommend that anyone with an interest in discovering more about the lesser known aspects of Luftwaffe history, as well as how Luftwaffe operations were traced by Allied signals intelligence, visit Nick Beale's website at www.ghostbombers.com which is a superb and fascinating resource. Nick's own research has been of invaluable help in retelling the intriguing story of the *Kommando Olga* mission of 23 January 1945.

I must also thank Marcel van Heijkop for his kind assistance and advice, as well the late Hans Altrogge, and Karl-Ernst Fara. Also, my thanks to Eddie Creek, Dave Wadman, Martin Streetly, Richard Carrick, Tomáš Poruba, Tony Holmes and Janusz Swiatlon, from whose contributions and help this book has benefited.

Aside from the present author's overview that you now hold in your hands, there is, sadly, something of a dearth in the historiography of the Ju 188. That said, histories of KGs 2 and 6 do exist, and, at the time of writing, we await the fruits of Marcel von Heijkop's research into the history of KG 66, which I have no doubt will be of considerable interest and value. I must also recommend Christoph Vernaleken and Martin Handig's exhaustive work on the Junkers Ju 388 for those wishing to read more on the progressive development of the Ju 188 design.

INDEX